SPIRIT OF LIBERTY

Liberty is love

Paul Garner

ALL BIBLICAL QUOTATIONS:

Scripture quotations taken from the New American Standard Bible (NASB), Copyright ©1960, 1962, 1963, 1968,1971, 1972, 1973,1975, 1977,1995 by The Lockman Foundation. Used by permission. Lockman.org

PANTHERA PUBLISHING
PANTHERAPUBLISHING.COM
STUART, FLORIDA

DEDICATION

To God, the Author of Liberty and lover of our souls

CONTENTS

PREFACE

Since this book is largely addressed to Christians, it is no surprise that the core foundation of this book comes from the Bible. Christians for most of 2000 years have believed that the Bible is the Word of God containing the words of God as He inspired many writers to record them through the centuries. We accept the Bible as the infallible Word and words of God, the Creator of all things, who is eternal, righteous, merciful, compassionate, and loving. We take it as normative to seek His Word to know His character, His values, His purposes, and His will. We accept that Jesus is the perfect image of the invisible God, One with the Father, and through whom all things were created. We also accept that upon Jesus' ascension to the Father, His Holy Spirit was sent to dwell in His followers by faith and reveal the Father and the Son.

If you have read my first book, Yearning to Breathe Free, you will notice some overlapping material here. Nevertheless, some repetition of fundamental concepts is often helpful in building a strong foundation. I hope that you will bear with me in this process.

The purpose here is to re-examine God's Word and listen to His Spirit as He reveals to us God's intention in regard to how He planned for us to live, especially in regard to liberty. Over the centuries Christians have swung back and forth from weak and powerless to brutal authoritarians. I do not believe that either of these conditions are how God intended us to live.

While in Bible College, a professor challenged my fellow students and I to consider if a question or principle was truly scriptural or actually just cultural. This is a dilemma that many aspiring students of the Word have faced, sometimes leading to terrible error. Midway through the last century the author, Charles Sheldon, wrote the book In His Steps. Soon after the book was published the question circulated among Christians, "What would Jesus do?". The book inspired Christians to consider how faithful they were walking in Jesus' teaching about mercy, grace, integrity, purpose, and salvation. These are all very important indeed. Yet as we look at the scriptures and see the plan of God, we must ask ourselves 'how did we miss His value of liberty?' We will look directly to the scriptures examining them in a way that reveals God's original plan regarding liberty and then examining how we should walk in light of this. We can then ask the question again, "What would Jesus do?" as we see others through the lens of liberty which is the lens of love.

INTRODUCTION

Liberty is like money. Most Christians agree that the money and resources we have come from God and should be treated with wisdom and stewardship. This often requires focus and attention and discipline to earn well, save well, spend well, and give well. Liberty is like that too. Liberty is a gift from God. He values liberty so much that He put his whole creation at risk of the choice made by Adam and Eve to obey or not regarding the tree of the knowledge of good and evil. He knew what they would do. He knew what the results would be, and He made a way for redemption.

Liberty is also His gift that came with the founding of America. He inspired men and women of great courage to found a nation on Liberty and Justice for all, trusting in God. These are God's values. He inspired men to write and adopt the Declaration of Independence and a Constitution to protect those values.

Since the beginning, God has had an enemy in Satan who seeks to destroy all that God loves, especially we whom He loves. This is also played out across every nation in the world where harming and defeating God's people and God's values are the enemy's ways of getting back against God.

Many Christians believe that we should not get involved in picking sides in politics. After all God has all things in control. However, the battles we are experiencing in America are not just politics. That is the surface and deception of the enemy. They are battles for life, liberty, and justice for all. We must take sides in this battle. The stakes are enormous. Life. Millions of babies are slaughtered every year by heartless cruelty. Authoritarians across the political spectrum are rising more boldly to seize our God given liberties and our earnings. Social justice warriors are claiming justice for themselves in forcing the people of God to live contrary to God's Word and Spirit. We must take sides against these things just as the founders, following God, took sides against the oppressions of King George.

We must also understand ourselves as we are constantly deceived by the evil one into self-righteousness and into believing either that God does not want us to get involved or that He wants us to use force to defend His values and gain compliance by others. This is not how God has treated us nor has He modeled this for us.

Of course, the battle is not exclusively in the flesh. It is a spiritual battle that, to be truly effective, must be fought with spiritual weapons. The weapons of the armor of God, the helmet of salvation, the breastplate of righteousness, the shield of faith and the sword of truth. Our weapons also include prayer and fasting, declarations of authority and supernatural power in the Holy Spirit. We must engage the battle while we remain here, and we must understand that we are fighting the enemy of God who wants to strip us of our lives, liberty, and justice.

Yes. By all means, take sides. Engage the battle. Take a side, the side of life, liberty, and justice. God's side.

LIBERTY IS A GIFT FROM GOD.

GOD IS THE AUTHOR OF LIBERTY

In the Garden

> *Then the LORD God took the man and put him into the garden of Eden to cultivate it and keep it. The LORD God commanded the man, saying, "From any tree of the garden you may eat freely; but from the tree of the knowledge of good and evil you shall not eat, for in the day that you eat from it you will surely die." —Genesis 2:15–17*

In the opening chapters of Genesis, we encounter a profound paradox: God, who is all-powerful, all-knowing, and perfectly good, placed within the Garden of Eden a tree that He explicitly warned His created humans not to eat from—a tree that would ultimately serve as the catalyst for human sin, suffering, and death.

To the modern mind, especially one raised in the atmosphere of suspicion toward religious authority, this seems contradictory. Why would a loving God place such a dangerous tree within reach and then leave the humans with the freedom to choose wrongly? Wouldn't a benevolent creator have removed the possibility of disobedience altogether?

But this question reveals more about our discomfort with liberty than it does about God's intentions.

God is not an authoritarian. He is the author of liberty.

By placing the Tree of the Knowledge of Good and Evil in the garden and giving a clear boundary, not a barricade, God extended to Adam and Eve something radical: trust. He trusted His creatures with freedom. This act of trust forms the foundation of the biblical vision of liberty. It is not a coerced obedience that God desires, but a voluntary relationship of trust and love, built on the ability to choose.

To be made in the image of God is to be free. Freedom is the raw material of love. Without liberty, love is not love at all, but compulsion. And God, who is love, created us not as robots or slaves but as sovereign beings—bearing responsibility, agency, and the sacred dignity of choice.

MISUNDERSTANDING GOD'S AUTHORITY

Many people, even Christians, carry an image of God as a cosmic dictator. They imagine Him keeping a long list of moral infractions, punishing those who break His rules and rewarding those who comply. Often, this image is shaped more by human institutions than by divine revelation.

Over the centuries, religious communities have added layers of rules and traditions, some rooted in scripture, many not. Prohibitions on alcohol, dancing, playing cards, certain music styles, dress codes, and even medical practices have all been justified in the name of holiness. These added burdens can make God appear more like an authoritarian parent than a loving Father.

Take, for example, the experience of Hudson Armerding, former president of Wheaton College. In the 1960s and 70s, as rock and roll rose in popularity, many Christian parents feared its influence, calling it "devil's music." Ironically, Armerding himself had once believed the same about jazz in the 1920s and 30s when he was young. Each generation has its own cultural fears, and each generation is tempted to declare their preferences as divine imperatives.

This human impulse—to take our convictions and universalize them under the banner of God's authority—is one of the oldest forms of legalism. But legalism is not liberty, and it is not of God.

The Garden of Eden tells a different story. There, God gave Adam and Eve access to everything except one tree. Not because He was arbitrary or insecure, but because love without choice is not love.

WHY THE TREE? WHY THE RISK?

Many have asked, "If God didn't want Adam and Eve to eat from that tree, why put it there at all?"

The answer lies in the nature of love and liberty. True freedom always includes the possibility of failure. A world where no wrong can be chosen is also a world where choosing right is not a true choice either. For obedience to have any moral value, it must be voluntary. For love to be genuine, it must be freely given.

God, in His sovereignty, subjected all of creation to the possibility of futility. As Paul writes in Romans 8:

> *"For the creation was subjected to futility, not willingly, but because of Him who subjected it, in hope that the creation itself also will be set free from its slavery to corruption into the freedom of the glory of the children of God." —Romans 8:20–21*

This is staggering. God didn't merely allow liberty; He designed the cosmos to accommodate it. And not shallow liberty, not the kind of "liberty" where you're free to choose as long as you choose what's approved, but deep, dangerous, soul-shaping liberty. The liberty to reject Him. The liberty to destroy what He made. The liberty to bring death into the world.

And He did it all for the sake of love.

THE CONSEQUENCES OF LIBERTY

The liberty to choose is a double-edged sword. When Adam and Eve chose disobedience, they opened the floodgates of suffering—not just for themselves, but for all of creation. This is a sobering truth.

> *"Just as through one man sin entered into the world, and death through sin, and so death spread to all men, because all sinned." —Romans 5:12*

Their decision shattered the harmony of the created order. The earth itself began to groan. Thorns and thistles erupted from the ground. Pain entered childbirth. Labor became toil. Death became inevitable.

But notice: God did not revoke their liberty even then. He allowed them to suffer the consequences of their choices, but He did not reclaim their agency. In fact, after their disobedience, He clothed them (Genesis 3:21), demonstrating that while liberty may bring pain, it does not remove the possibility of redemption.

This is the rhythm of liberty in God's Kingdom: permission, consequence, grace.

SPIRITUAL DEATH AND THE FRAGMENTED SELF

Some wonder, "If God said they would die on the day they ate from the tree, why didn't they die physically?" The answer lies in understanding death not only as a physical event but as a spiritual disconnection.

Humans are composed of body, soul, and spirit. The body is our physical form, the soul includes our emotions and intellect, and the spirit is the deepest part of us—the part that communes with God.

When Adam and Eve disobeyed, their bodies continued to live. Their minds and personalities were intact. But their spirits were severed from God. This spiritual death was immediate and devastating. They were suddenly aware of their nakedness. Shame was born. Fear entered the human vocabulary.

Cut off from God's presence, their souls were left to govern themselves. And ever since, humanity has been navigating the world with a broken compass—relying on self-interest, instinct, and power, rather than spiritual union with the Creator.

THE CURSED GROUND AND THE STRUGGLE OF MAN

> *"Cursed is the ground because of you; in toil you shall eat of it all the days of your life."* —Genesis 3:17

Another consequence of the Fall was the corruption of creation itself. Not just spiritual death, but ecological disarray. The ground would resist cultivation. Nature, once harmonious, became hostile. Man's dominion over the earth turned from joyful stewardship into painful labor.

This wasn't just punishment. It was reality. Liberty brings consequence. The same liberty that allows love also allows ruin. God could have prevented it all. He could have made Adam and Eve incapable of disobedience. But in doing so, He would have erased their humanity.

Instead, He allowed them to be fully human and in doing so, He opened the door for us to understand the gravity, beauty, and cost of liberty.

Genesis 3:16 adds yet another layer to the curse:

"Your desire will be for your husband, and he will rule over you."

This verse has been misused throughout history to justify patriarchy and oppression. But it is not a prescription. It is a description of what happens when relationships are no longer governed by God's Spirit.

In the pre-Fall world, Adam and Eve were partners. There was no hierarchy, no exploitation. Their unity reflected the very image of God. But after the Fall, domination entered the picture. Desire, control, rivalry, and mistrust began to infect the human relationship.

Even our most intimate bonds became battlegrounds for power. And again, this is a consequence of liberty being misused.

We sometimes fear liberty because we fear what others will do with it. We fear that if people are left free, they will harm, destroy, or rebel. And history has many examples to support that fear. But God knew this risk, and still chose liberty.

God's design has always included the possibility of failure. What would the world look like if all people were truly free? That question haunts some. But in Eden, God gave us the answer: it would be dangerous. And it would be worth it.

God's Kingdom does not flourish under compulsion. It grows through invitation, response, trust, and transformation. Even when Israel demanded a king like the nations (1 Samuel 8), God warned them of the consequences but allowed it. Liberty is woven into the DNA of His governance.

THE TREE OF LIFE AND THE HOPE OF REDEMPTION

In the garden stood another tree—the Tree of Life. It was not forbidden. In fact, after the Fall, God expelled Adam and Eve from Eden not out of vengeance, but to prevent them from eating of the Tree of Life in their fallen state and living forever in separation (Genesis 3:22–24).

Even in judgment, God was merciful. He protected them from eternal alienation. And the Tree of Life is not gone forever. It reappears in the final pages of Scripture:

> *"On either side of the river was the tree of life...*
> *and the leaves of the tree were for the healing of*
> *the nations." —Revelation 22:2*

From the first garden to the New Jerusalem, liberty and love remain God's plan. Humanity's journey begins with freedom misused, but it ends with freedom restored.

God could have created a world without danger, without sin, without risk. But He created something better, a world where love is real, because liberty is real.

The Garden of Eden was not a trap. It was a test. A sacred space where God's image-bearers were invited to trust, to obey, to love. They failed. And so have we.

But the story of Scripture is the story of a God who does not revoke liberty even when it is abused. Instead, He redeems. Through Christ , the second Adam, He restores what was lost. He breathes life back into our spirits. He opens the door to fellowship again. He invites us back to the garden, not as captives, but as children.

Liberty is not the absence of boundaries. It is the presence of trust.

In the beginning, God trusted humanity with freedom. And in Christ, He has done so again.

LIBERTY IS LOVE

THE SEED OF AUTHORITARIANISM

When they grew up, Abel became a shepherd, while Cain cultivated the ground. When it was time for the harvest, Cain presented some of his crops as a gift to the LORD. Abel also brought a gift—the best portions of the firstborn lambs from his flock. The LORD accepted Abel and his gift, but he did not accept Cain and his gift. This made Cain very angry, and he looked dejected. "Why are you so angry?" the LORD asked Cain. "Why do you look so dejected? You will be accepted if you do what is right. But if you refuse to do what is right, then watch out! Sin is crouching at the door, eager to control you. But you must subdue it and be its master."

One day Cain suggested to his brother, "Let's go out into the fields." And while they were in the field, Cain attacked his brother, Abel, and killed him. Afterward, the LORD asked Cain, "Where is your brother? Where is Abel?" "I don't know," Cain responded. "Am I my brother's guardian?"

But the LORD said, "What have you done? Listen! Your brother's blood cries out to me from the ground! Now you are cursed and banished from the ground, which has swallowed your brother's blood. No longer will the ground yield good crops for you, no matter how hard you work! From now on you will be a homeless wanderer on the earth. - Genesis 4:2-12

Few people consider the impact of that lost connection from God in terms of human character. Very soon after being banished from the garden, we find people involved in murder. The selfish blindness of rage and revenge enveloped Cain as he struck down his brother. In God's punishment, Cain became afraid that someone else would strike him down. Killing and murder quickly became common among people.

Other character flaws arose among those early humans as well. Number one among them was fear. No longer did they have the connection with God that brought peace and trust. Fear led them to seek control of their environment and circumstances and other people. Their fear led them to murder, assault and theft. Their fear led them to control others, to authoritarianism and to reject the liberty that God had given them.

When Cain killed Abel, he was acting as an authoritarian, believing that he was justified in his actions. He was offended when God regarded Abel's offering over his. Rather than taking a repentant and humble approach, he chose the path of pride and self-justification and seizing the life of Abel by power, destroying it.

Secondary to fear in some people was the pure avarice for power over others for selfish ambition. Murders, abuses, thefts increased as those who believed that they were justified in these things abounded. Some were elevated to kings and rulers who used their belief in their own superiority to wage authoritarian and totalitarian actions against subjects, conquered peoples, and sometimes even their own households.

This wickedness among men continued for about 1000 years to the time of the flood.

> *Then the LORD saw that the wickedness of man was great on the earth, and that every intent of the thoughts of his heart was only evil continually.* -Genesis 6:5

The word "saw" in this context indicates that God was looking over a long human period, patient with the humans. The reference to "great" portrays something non-trivial, something widespread and firmly rooted in the minds and hearts of people.

Later, many people read into this the idea of immoral sexuality but evil extends far beyond that. Slavery. Theft. Brutalization. Coercion. Intimidation. Lies. All of these are fruits of authoritarianism. The drive to control others for selfish reasons. The belief by people that they are justified in their actions by right of power, fear, or their personal definition of morality.

> *For out of the heart come evil thoughts, murders, adulteries, fornications, thefts, false witness, slanders.* - Matthew 15:19

REJECTION OF GOD'S LIBERTY

Many Christians wish that temptation did not exist. Everyone has been tempted through their lives and surrendered to that temptation randomly. Due to the feelings of defeat and even calamity that can come from choices made for destructive things, many people wish that the subject of their temptation did not exist, that they did not have the opportunity to choose it. Worse still, they begin to believe that love means removing the objects of temptation from themselves and others so that they would not fall to those choices. This is not God's way.

If you were asked the question, "what is the greatest gift God gave us?", what would your response be? Many will respond that the greatest gift is life. Others may say that the greatest gift is Jesus as He gave His life for us. Consider, though, what value those would be if we did not have the liberty to choose. A slave has life but cannot choose freely. The benefits of Jesus' sacrifice of His life are received by choice. We must choose to believe in Him and His sacrifice for us to enter the Kingdom of God. Without liberty this would not be possible. Without liberty we could not be responsible for our sin. Jesus' sacrifice would have been in vain.

SO, YOU WANT TO GO BACK TO EGYPT?

> *The whole congregation of the sons of Israel grumbled against Moses and Aaron in the wilderness. The sons of Israel said to them, "Would that we had died by the LORD'S hand in the land of Egypt, when we sat by the pots of meat, when we ate bread to the full; for you have brought us out into this wilderness to kill this whole assembly with hunger." -Exodus 16:2-3*

Few Christians can imagine that they would be like the people of Israel who grumbled against Moses even after he had led them out of extremely oppressive slavery and hardship. However, this story is repeated often with the people of God when they reject God and the liberty that He provides and voluntarily choose slavery to a human king or government who abuses them. Somehow the unknown or uncertainty of trusting in God is more to be feared than the certainty of familiar slavery.

NO KING IN ISRAEL

Twice in the book of Judges the author says,

> *"In those days there was no king in Israel; every man did what was right in his own eyes." Judges 17:6 and 21:25.*

Many Christians who do not understand how God values liberty look at this verse and see it as a description of something shameful and awful, a rejection of God. Yet this was the condition that existed before the Law was given to Moses. Read Job and see that he honored God and humbled himself before God but there was no law forcing him to do so. There was no punishment if he did not do these things. Job did what was right in his own eyes. Similarly with Abraham. There was no law or government forcing him to trust and obey God. God did not force him to uproot his family and travel far away for a land he did not know about. Abraham already had a relationship with God such that he knew that he could trust God. Abraham did what was right in his own eyes. He trusted God without fear or coercion.

When God gave the Law to Moses to give to the people, each one had the liberty to reject that law. Each man retained the right to do what he wanted in his own eyes. When a man harmed another man or woman or donkey, the judges were there to judge between the man and those he harmed. However, there was no government other than the judges and God. After the people moved into the promised land and spread out, it was up to each man to do what was right in his own eyes based on his knowledge and acceptance of the covenant law given through Moses. No roaming enforcement to inspect for compliance to the law existed. Yes there were specified consequences for offenses of the law. However, unless a community member brought a charge to a judge with at least 2 witnesses, there would be no enforcement. God expected each man to do what was right in light of their knowledge of the law in the Covenant. That is, *in their own eyes*.

Many Christians believe how terrible that every man should be able to do what is right in his own eyes. After all, we know what happened with Adam and Eve, Cain and Abel, and the generations since. This is a common reaction even among Christians in America. They fear liberty. They fear what their neighbor might do. For them, liberty means only anarchy. They associate liberty with sin and rejection of God. They refuse to understand that liberty is the condition that God created for humans. God does not regret putting that tree in the garden. God does not regret giving Adam and Eve that choice. He did not make a mistake. It was His design for humans to have such choices and the opportunity to choose right from wrong.

CHOOSING A KING

For over 250 years the people of Israel lived at liberty. Daily they were faced with the same choice as Adam and Eve, to obey God or not. While there were judges to resolve disputes between people, there is no record of law enforcement beyond the family or clan. It was up to each person to obey the laws of the nation and up to their neighbors to carry out any punishment accorded in the law. Over time, as compliance with God's laws declined, God withdrew His protection and blessings. This led to war and subjection to the authoritarianism of other nations who conquered, enslaved and abused them.

This cycle repeats many times until the people simply decide that the liberty that God provided was too difficult to live with. They decided that the authoritarian commands of an earthly King are preferable to the liberty of choice.

> *"Then all the elders of Israel gathered together and came to Samuel at Ramah; and they said to him, "Behold, you have grown old, and your sons do not walk in your ways. Now appoint a king for us to judge us like all the nations." But the thing was displeasing in the sight of Samuel when they said, "Give us a king to judge us." And Samuel prayed to the LORD. The LORD said to Samuel, "Listen to the voice of the people in regard to all that they say to you, for they have not rejected*

you, but they have rejected Me from being king over them."

- 1 Samuel 8:4-7

They reject God from being King over them with all the liberty that came with that. God pointed out to them what it will be like to have such an earthly King.

"This will be the procedure of the king who will reign over you: he will take your sons and place them for himself in his chariots and among his horsemen and they will run before his chariots. He will appoint for himself commanders of thousands and of fifties, and some to do his plowing and to reap his harvest and to make his weapons of war and equipment for his chariots. He will also take your daughters for perfumers and cooks and bakers. He will take the best of your fields and your vineyards and your olive groves and give them to his servants. He will take a tenth of your seed and of your vineyards and give it to his officers and to his servants. He will also take your male servants and your female servants and your best young men and your donkeys and use them for his work. He will take a tenth of your flocks, and you yourselves will become his servants. Then you will cry out in that day because of your king whom you have chosen for yourselves, but the LORD will not answer you in that day."

Nevertheless, the people refused to listen to the voice of Samuel, and they said, "No, but there shall be a king over us, that we also may be like all the nations, that our king may judge us and go out before us and fight our battles."

-1 Samuel 8:11-20

From that day, the people of Israel became slaves to their earthly king. God did not make this choice for them. They chose it. God gave them that liberty to choose and honored their choice. He gave them over to the desires of their hearts and the consequences that come with that.

A vast majority of Christians have rejected God's liberty. Christians have put their trust in human government over God and sought the safety of that not realizing till it is too late that that is an illusion. They have accepted the confiscation of their earnings, the limitations on their commerce and labor, the regulation and theft of their property. They have embraced and even supported requirements for permissions (licensing) for marriage, operating a business, fishing, and offering labor services such as hair styling, home carpentry, and how they may use their own property, etc. Our government spies on us, lies to us, advocates the murder of our children, teaches our children to violate God's design in their bodies, and corrupts them with pornography.

MORE LAWS

It is generally accepted that the original laws given to Moses by God number about 613. This is not absolute in that few can clearly identify each one. We can, however, find many in the Torah or Pentateuch, the first 5 books of the Bible. These are the laws that God gave to the people of Israel through Moses to live by.

As noted previously, over time the people grew to ignore many or most of these, leading to cycles of subjection to foreign powers and authorities. They decide that an earthly king would be the right choice to reduce or eliminate these cycles and provide a better, common defense against foreign powers and authorities.

Over a thousand years, the people are slaves either to their own kings or to the kings of foreign powers. The Biblical text reveals the history of this idea as king after king reigns. Some are good and obey God's Covenant and laws. Others do not. Civil war splits the country into north and south. Their kings have various successes defending against foreign powers. The people benefit or suffer from the ambitions and sins of their kings. Even King David, a man after God's own heart, whom God anointed as king, brought great suffering on the people from his own ambition and sin. He takes another man's wife and has her husband murdered.

> *Now when evening came David arose from his bed and walked around on the roof of the king's house, and from the roof he saw a woman bathing; and the woman was very beautiful in appearance. So, David sent and inquired about the woman. And one said, "Is this not Bathsheba, the daughter of Eliam, the wife of Uriah the Hittite?" David sent messengers and took her, and when she came to him, he lay with her; - 2 Samuel 11:2-4*

> *Now in the morning David wrote a letter to Joab and sent it by the hand of Uriah. He had written in the letter, saying, "Place Uriah in the front line of the fiercest battle and withdraw from him, so that he may be struck down and die. - 2 Samuel 11:14-15*

Later, he sets about counting the people in a census. This leads to a plague on the people and seventy thousand of the people die.

> *Nevertheless, the king's word prevailed against Joab and against the commanders of the army. So Joab and the commanders of the army went out from the presence of the king to register the people of Israel. - 2 Samuel 24:4*

> *So the LORD sent a pestilence upon Israel from the morning until the appointed time, and seventy thousand men of the people from Dan to Beersheba died. - 2 Samuel 24:15*

Finally, the nation is reduced to a shadow of itself through civil war, foreign wars, and captivities. Only a portion of the southern kingdom is restored.

After this time, in an effort to limit the option of breaking God's laws, religious sects created new laws to govern the people to keep them from breaking God's given laws. In order to ensure that no one should violate the sabbath by working, they created new laws limiting how many steps one could walk on the sabbath. As we know from the gospels, they even found fault with Jesus healing on the sabbath.

> *And He was teaching in one of the synagogues on the Sabbath. And there was a woman who for eighteen years had had a sickness caused by a spirit; and she was bent double, and could not straighten up at all. When Jesus saw her, He called her over and said to her, "Woman, you are freed from your sickness." And He laid His hands on her; and immediately she was made erect again and began glorifying God. But the synagogue official, indignant because Jesus had healed on the Sabbath, began saying to the crowd in response, "There are six days in which work should be done; so come during them and get healed, and not on the Sabbath day." But the Lord answered him and said, "You hypocrites, does not each of you on the Sabbath untie his ox or his donkey from the stall and lead him away to water him? And this woman, a daughter of Abraham as she is, whom Satan has bound for eighteen long*

years, should she not have been released from this bond on the Sabbath day?" As He said this, all His opponents were being humiliated; and the entire crowd was rejoicing over all the glorious things being done by Him. - Luke 13:10-17

These very many laws became an enormous burden on the people.

Jesus reminded the people that the laws were created by God to serve people not to enslave them. He reminded them of what David did when he and his followers were hungry and went into the house of God and ate the consecrated bread which was unlawful. David was not condemned as a law breaker.

*And it happened that He was passing through the grainfields on the Sabbath, and His disciples began to make their way along while picking the heads of grain. The Pharisees were saying to Him, "Look, why are they doing what is not lawful on the Sabbath?" And He *said to them, "Have you never read what David did when he was in need and he and his companions became hungry; how he entered the house of God in the time of Abiathar the high priest, and ate the consecrated bread, which is not lawful for anyone to eat except the priests, and he also gave it to those who were with him?" Jesus said to them, "The Sabbath was made for man, and not man for the Sabbath. So the Son of Man is Lord even of the Sabbath."* Mark 2:23-28

When people do not obey His laws, God's solution is not to create more laws. The apostle, Paul, tells us that God gives people "over" to their own lusts and desires.

Therefore God gave them over in the lusts of their hearts Romans 1:24

For this reason God gave them over to degrading passions Romans 1:26

God gave them over to a depraved mind, to do those things which are not proper Romans 1:28

This means that He does not stop them from making foolish and sinful choices. He allows them to "receive in their own persons the penalty of their error".

GOD IS NOT AN AUTHORITARIAN

But humans often are. The fall from the condition of favor in the garden often describes the changes in the character of humanity but few describe the rise of authoritarianism.

Authoritarians are constantly seeking to increase laws and rules. Some are canonized into a national register. Some are common laws of a society that change over time. Some are simply the preferences of authoritarians, i.e., "there oughta be a law", prohibiting what they don't approve and requiring or forcing what they do. The worst kind are those who seek to create laws and social mores to enforce their own view of morality.

"Of all tyrannies, a tyranny sincerely exercised for the good of its victims may be the most oppressive. It would be better to live under robber barons than under omnipotent moral busybodies. The robber baron's cruelty may sometimes sleep, his cupidity may at some point be satiated; but

those who torment us for our own good will torment us without end for they do so with the approval of their own conscience. "– C.S. Lewis[1]

It is clear from scripture and from history that all humans have an authoritarian streak originating with the fall from the garden along with the rest of our nature to sin. When we act as authoritarians, seeking to control others, then we are acting contrary to God's character and purposes. It is His plan that we walk according to His plan and leave others to choose how they will walk. We have no authority from God to remove temptation and choice from anyone's path.

_____

[1] God in the Dock: Essays on Theology (Making of Modern Theology), CS Lewis

WHAT IS LIBERTY?

LIBERTY VS FREEDOM

These words are often used interchangeably as if they mean the same thing and to many they do. The actual definitions of these words are not universally agreed upon.

The Oxford English dictionary has these definitions for liberty.

1) The condition of being free from confinement, servitude, or forced labor.

2) The condition of being free from oppressive restriction or control by a government or other power.

3) A right to engage in certain actions without control or interference by a government or other power.

4) The right or power to act as one chooses.

And these for Freedom

1) The condition of not being in prison or captivity

2) The condition of being free of restraints, especially the ability to act without control or interference by another or by circumstance

3) The condition of not being constrained or restricted in a specific aspect of life by a government or other power

4) The condition of not being bound by established conventions or rules

5) The capacity to act by choice rather than by determination, as from fate or a deity

As you can see, based on this dictionary, the definitions are remarkably similar and overlap in many respects.

However, I believe that Brian Miller of the Liberty Beacon provides a better and perhaps more nuanced explanation of the differences.

> *"Freedom" is predominantly an internal construct. Viktor Frankl, the legendary Holocaust survivor who wrote <u>Man's Search For Meaning</u>, said it well: "Everything can be taken from a man but one thing: the last of the human freedoms – to choose one's attitude in any given set of*

circumstances, to choose one's own way (in how he approaches his circumstances)."

In other words, to be free is to take ownership of what goes on between your ears, to be autonomous in thoughts first and actions second. Your freedom to act a certain way can be taken away from you – but your attitude about your circumstances cannot – making one's freedom predominantly an internal construct.

On the other hand, "liberty" is predominantly an external construct. It's the state of being free within society from oppressive restrictions imposed by authority on one's way of life, behavior, or political views. The ancient Stoics knew this. So did the Founding Fathers, who wisely noted the distinction between negative and positive liberties and codified that difference in the U.S. Constitution and Bill of Rights." [1]

It is evident through history that many people are deceived into believing that freedom and liberty are something else altogether.

"We and all others who believe in freedom as deeply as we do, would rather die on our feet than live on our knees." Franklin Roosevelt. While we may agree with Roosevelt on this, anyone who has read history would have to agree that he did not define this as we do.

Jesus said, *"If you continue in My word, then you are truly disciples of Mine; and you will know the truth, and the truth will make you free."* John 8:31-32

Clearly, He was referring to a freedom of the soul not of the body. He frees our soul from slavery to fear and to evil spirits and resurrects our spirit to reconnect with God as we were intended to live. This doesn't automatically free us if we are subject to physical slavery of our bodies that come from authoritarians and despots, whether in govt or society. This liberty allows us to choose our thoughts, feelings, and attitudes.

To summarize, freedom is mostly a function of our mind, emotions, and will. It is a function of thinking, choosing, and even willing ourselves. Liberty is largely an external condition or experience. Forces outside ourselves may exert power over us, coercing and limiting us. Liberty is the absence of such coercion or limitations.

Nevertheless, restrictions in external liberty can and very often do influence our mind, emotions and will, our soul. The poem on the foundation of the Statue of Liberty, "The New Colossus" by Emma Lazarus, describes a people "yearning to breathe free". This is an internal drive influenced by external restrictions in their home of origin leading to the external actions of seeking a different home with fewer external limitations. Early American settlers and pioneers continually moved west seeking this liberty from authoritarians seeking to control their lives that continually arose as communities grew. This drive, this desire to breathe free is the desire for liberty and comes from God's design. Out of fear and lack of trust in God many people deny this desire. Even fewer are willing to risk the actions to seek it. For those that do and find it, there is nothing greater for the human life.

Liberty is the greatest good. We know this because we bestow our greatest honors on those who give their lives for it and more. Even the signers of the American Declaration of Independence in 1776 declared in defense of liberty:

> *And for the support of this declaration, with a firm reliance on the protection of Divine Providence,*

we mutually pledge to each other our lives, our fortunes, and our sacred honor.

SOVEREIGNTY

Central to any understanding of liberty is the application of sovereignty. Sovereignty comes from the French word suzerain or souverain meaning highest, supreme, chief. This sovereign has the highest authority over something or someone. We often associate this with a king or emperor whose authority is ultimate and unquestionable.

> *"Through the Earth, and all inferior creatures, be common to all men, yet every man has a property in his own person. This, nobody has any right to but himself. The labor of his body and the work of his hands, we may say, are properly his. "*
>
> *-John Locke[2]*

Body

Each of us is born with a body and for a time our parents have the highest authority over us. At some point, usually approaching adulthood, liberty demands that we assume sovereignty over our own bodies. This sovereignty allows us and requires us to make our own choices as to what we put into our bodies, what activities we engage in with our bodies, how we care and maintain our bodies, and how we may terminate our bodies.

John Locke makes it clear that everyone has a sovereign right to their own body.

Understand, this does not support abortion or killing of babies. The baby is another, human life, deserving of the same right to life as its mother. The collective must have authority to defend one person's liberty from harm by another, including the unborn life carried by a mother.

Labor

John Locke again makes it clear that the labor of a body belongs to the owner of that body.

As sovereign over our bodies, we choose if we will labor or starve, what kind of labor we may engage in, and under what conditions. If the opportunities for our conditions and the type of labor, we desire are not available we still must choose if we will change our conditions or type of labor or starve. Our sovereignty remains but we may need to negotiate with the sovereignty of others seeking to contract our labor.

Liberty demands that we set the boundaries of our labor. No other sovereignty has any rightful authority over the boundaries of our labor except for that which interferes in the sovereignty of another.

Limitations of labor that does not harm anyone by government are contrary to natural law and by extension God's law.

Earnings

The earnings arising from our labor exist under our sovereignty and our liberty. The individual determines how the earnings are spent or distributed. Any attempts by any other authority to limit or confiscate those earnings without each individual's consent is theft and hostile to liberty. It matters not if a majority of a society decides to delegate authority to a sovereign other than the individual to regulate or confiscate these earnings. Any actions by any individual or collective to override consent is theft and assault.

Property

Finally, all purchases from our earnings originate from sovereignty over our bodies, and our body's labor, and the resulting earnings as the fruit of our labor. All individuals with their own sovereign property are free to offer it for sale or exchange to anyone else who is willing to pay from their own earnings.

Liberty demands no interference in the free exchange between individuals. Any coercive exchange by the buyer or seller is theft and assault. This is the only foundation for the society to interfere. Liberty demands sovereignty over the exchange by those willing and able to consent.

All forms of government taxation and regulation of private property are forced confiscation of that property and demonstrates, contrary to natural law, that they own all property. The individual does not. This is immoral This is a violation of our natural God-given rights.

NEGATIVE AND POSITIVE RIGHTS

There are two kinds of rights found in liberty. Negative rights mean freedom from interference. This is also known as the right to be left alone, to exist, to think, to say, to work, to create, to buy and sell. For example, suppose you decide to put a pool in your backyard, a property that you own. You have a negative right or liberty from your neighbor's interference. Negative rights also mean that your neighbor cannot be forced to help you with the pool. This can also be found in a right to free speech. You are free to speak as you wish. However, no one can be forced to provide a platform for you to speak nor can they be forced to listen to you. Negative rights are found in both the Declaration of Independence and Bill of Rights. "...certain inalienable rights, among which are life, liberty, and the pursuit of happiness". The Bill of Rights itemizes, through the amendments, negative rights as in "the government shall make no law abridging" the freedom of speech, religion, assembly, ownership of guns, etc. Citizens are to be free from illegal searches and seizures, from testifying against themselves, from housing soldiers in their home.

Positive rights, in contrast, entitle one to certain items or benefits. This is where authoritarians and progressives go wild. They will tell you that healthcare is a human right, as is a minimum or living wage, and education and should be provided free of charge to the receiver. This would be similar to forcing someone to help build a platform for you to speak. However, how is it possible that someone can have a positive right to something that requires or forces someone else to provide it? In fact, if someone has a positive right to a good or service then by definition someone else has a positive responsibility to deliver it even if without compensation. The negative rights of one person are violated in the force of providing a positive right to someone else.

The Bill of Rights actually does have a few instances of positive rights. A Right to a speedy, jury trial (6th amendment), to be confronted by witnesses, and to be provided with an attorney. These cost the taxpayers to provide and so a coercive measure is applied, forced compliance. This becomes the open door for progressives to add on many other so-called rights that are paid for by the coercive power of the government.

———

[1]https://www.thelibertybeacon.com/freedom-vs-liberty-how-subtle-differences-between-these-two-big-ideas-changed-our-world/

[2]Of Property and Government, John Locke, Sec 27, 1689

RESTRAINT OF POWER

> *Therefore, God gave them over in the lusts of their hearts to impurity, so that their bodies would be dishonored among them. For they exchanged the truth of God for a lie and worshiped and served the creature rather than the Creator, who is blessed forever. Amen.*
> *Romans 1:24-25*

What scripture is telling us here is that God restrains His power over all people just as He did with Adam and Eve. God is not an authoritarian. He allows people to make their own choices even when they may be self-destructive. He strongly desires that people make good, positive, righteous, even obedient choices but He knows better than we do that we will not always do that. Yes, we are likely to experience negative consequences from our choices and His mercy and presence will be there too. He will be with us even in the consequences of our choices. That is what love looks like. Love DOES NOT remove the opportunity for bad choices, but love can be present alongside us in our consequences. Just as God does not always save us from those consequences, we must follow His example. It may not be our place to save others from earthly, physical consequences.

In the above verses from Romans, Paul is addressing homosexuality, but this could easily be applied to other desires of people not in line with God's values and plans such as when the people of Israel desired a human King. God gave them over to their desires even after warning them of what it will be like for them to have a human king.

> *The LORD said to Samuel, "Listen to the voice of the people in regard to all that they say to you, for they have not rejected you, but they have rejected Me from being king over them. [8] Like all the deeds which they have done since the day that I brought them up from Egypt even to this day—in that they have forsaken Me and served other gods—so they are doing to you also. Now then, listen to their voice; however, you shall solemnly warn them and tell them of the procedure of the king who will reign over them. "*

> *So Samuel spoke all the words of the LORD to the people who had asked of him a king. [11] He said, "This will be the procedure of the king who will reign over you: he will take your sons and place them for himself in his chariots and among his horsemen and they will run before his chariots. [12] He will appoint for himself commanders of thousands and of fifties, and some to do his plowing and to reap his harvest and to make his weapons of war and equipment for his chariots. [13] He will also take your daughters for perfumers and cooks and bakers. [14] He will take the best of your fields and your vineyards and your olive groves and give them to his servants. [15] He will take a tenth of your seed and of your vineyards and give to his officers and to his servants. [16] He will also take your male servants and your female servants and your best young men and your donkeys and use them for his work. [17] He will take a tenth of your flocks, and you yourselves will become his servants. [18] Then you will cry out in that day*

because of your king whom you have chosen for
yourselves, but the LORD will not answer you in
that day." 1 Samuel 8:7-18

Note here that God is drawing a contrast of a human king vs Himself as King. The human king is an authoritarian, self-interested and entitled. Even David, a man after God's heart, fell from a humble place to a place of pride, selfishness and entitlement leading to adultery and murder. While the scripture doesn't tell us fully, we can safely understand that this list of things that God warned the people about a king are the same things that David did. After all he was a human king. God did not prevent David or Solomon or any king from acting sinfully. God is not an authoritarian.

The history of the kings of Israel from that point is mixed but mostly dark. They often led the people astray from following God and into the worship of other gods. Of course, God knew that this would happen, and He allowed it anyway by restraining His own power out of love. Love does not override someone's desires or choices. Love patiently waits until they discover the consequences of their desires and return.

Even as Jesus was standing accused before Pilate, He again demonstrates restraint of His own power.

> *Therefore, when Pilate heard this statement, he*
> *was even more afraid; and he entered into the*
> *Praetorium again and *said to Jesus, "Where are*
> *You from?" But Jesus gave him no answer. So*
> *Pilate *said to Him, "You do not speak to me? Do*
> *You not know that I have authority to release You,*
> *and I have authority to crucify You?" Jesus*
> *answered, "You would have no authority over Me,*
> *unless it had been given you from above."*
>
> -John 19:8-11

Jesus would not even take the choice away from Pilate to sentence Him to death. Jesus is God. He cannot go against His own character. Liberty to choose is His highest value because liberty is love. In the same way as when God put the tree of the knowledge of good and evil in the garden, giving Adam and Eve a choice, He delivered His own Son up to the choice of people which continues even to this day.

> *He who did not spare His own Son, but delivered*
> *Him over for us all, how will He not also with Him*
> *freely give us all things?* - Romans 8:32

Consider that He actually restrains His power allowing us this liberty every day. We are faced with this choice often, to obey and walk in His ways or in our own desires. He is the author of liberty and restrains His power allowing us to follow our own desires and suffer the consequences. He provides us everything we need to make good, healthy, righteous choices through His Word and Spirit. He calls us to follow Him and obey Him but allows us the liberty to follow our own path and our own desires. He does not have to punish us for our choices. He allows us to reap what we sow from our choices. The fruit of our choices are often negative enough. How can we act differently toward other people?

What if our desires were for Him and His liberty? Would He exercise His power at our request in favor of liberty? In favor of righteousness and virtue.

ABRAHAM: THE BLESSING OF COVENANT AND LEGACY

Abraham's story is perhaps the most foundational narrative of obedience and blessing in the Old Testament. Called out of Ur to a land he did not know, Abraham responded in trust and obedience.

His journey begins with God's promise: "Go from your country...to the land that I will show you. I will make you into a great nation...and all peoples on earth will be blessed through you" (Genesis 12:1–3).

Abraham's obedience was not passive or easy. It required leaving everything familiar. He followed God into the unknown, faced famine, family disputes, war, and the long waiting of unfulfilled promise. Yet with each act of obedience—building altars, offering peace, believing God's word despite Sarah's barrenness—Abraham's life was marked by divine intervention and blessing.

The ultimate test came on Mount Moriah, where God asked him to offer his promised son Isaac. It is here that we see not only Abraham's obedience, but God's restraint of power. God could have demanded Isaac. He could have stopped the test before it began. But He allowed Abraham to walk through the choice so that Abraham—and we—might know the depth of obedient faith. At every point along the way Abraham was free to choose to obey or not. And once again, the response of heaven is unmistakable: "Because you have done this and have not withheld your son...I will surely bless you" (Genesis 22:16–17). The blessings of obedience in Abraham's life were not merely material or individual. They were generational and eternal—covenantal blessings that shaped the destiny of nations and pointed toward Christ.

JOB: THE BLESSING OF INTEGRITY AND RESTORATION

In contrast to Abraham, Job did not receive a call or command. He was not tested with a promise, but with the apparent silence of heaven in the face of suffering. Job's obedience was revealed not in action, but in reaction. It was forged in the crucible of loss and grief.

Satan challenged God, claiming that Job only served Him because of the blessings God had provided. God allowed the hedge to be lowered, not to punish Job, but to reveal that obedience grounded in love and reverence is not contingent on circumstance. Job lost his children, his wealth, his health, and even the confidence of his friends and wife. Yet he did not curse God. He questioned, wept, lamented, but he stayed in the conversation with God. "Though He slay me, yet will I hope in Him" (Job 13:15).

In Job's story, we find a deeper blessing of choosing to obey God, the blessing of integrity, the preservation of one's soul in the midst of chaos. Job's friends tried to frame obedience as transactional, "do good and God will bless you", but Job's steadfastness in his choice reveals something more enduring. Obedience is not a lever we pull to force God's hand, but a posture of the heart that anchors us in trust.

And yet, God does respond. He speaks. He restores. Not only does Job receive double what he had lost, but he also experiences the blessing of divine revelation. "My ears had heard of You," Job says, "but now my eyes have seen You" (Job 42:5). The greatest blessing Job receives is not wealth returned, but the intimacy gained through obedient faithfulness.

THE MOSAIC LAW: THE BLESSING OF ORDERED LIBERTY

The giving of the Mosaic Law is a remarkable moment where liberty and restraint intersect. God rescues Israel from Egypt not to enslave them anew, but to bring them into a covenantal relationship governed by law and liberty. The law is not given as a tool of domination but as a framework for flourishing—a revelation of God's character and the conditions for communal blessing.

In Deuteronomy 28, the blessings of obedience are laid out with clarity and abundance. "If you fully obey the Lord your God...all these blessings will come upon you and accompany you: You will be blessed in the city and blessed in the country...The Lord will establish you as His holy people...The Lord will open the heavens...to bless all the work of your hands" (Deuteronomy 28:1– 12).

THE PATTERN OF BLESSING THROUGH OBEDIENCE

In each of these stories, the pattern is clear. Abraham obeyed and received a promise that transcended time. Job obeyed and encountered a deeper knowledge of God. Israel was invited into a covenant of blessing through obedience to the law.

But even more profound is this truth: God's blessings are not rewards for performance; they are expressions of His character poured out on those who trust Him. Obedience opens the door to deeper relationship, clearer vision, and fuller participation in the purposes of God. Blessing is not always immediate or material, but it is always meaningful and eternal.

This principle resonates powerfully with the idea of divine restraint. God allows us to choose—just as Abraham could have said no, just as Job could have cursed God, just as Israel could (and often did) rebel. But with each step of obedience, the door to blessing opens wider—not because God is stingy, but because obedience aligns us with the flow of His will and goodness.

As we reflect on the restraint of God's power, may we also reflect on the opportunity that liberty gives us: to obey, to trust, and to walk in the blessings that flow from a heart yielded to Him.

Contrary to God, authoritarians insist that we live according to their desires. They take away options that might divert us from their plans. Consider what happened in the US during the 1920s. A group of activists, the "temperance movement", persuaded ¾ of

Americans, especially Christians that they should take away the option of producing and consuming alcohol. (The 18th Amendment to the Constitution.) Yes, some people abused alcohol but not everyone did. They were frustrated that persuasion was ineffective and so resorted to force. All legislation is force. They took away the choice of their fellow citizens. This turned many otherwise law-abiding Americans into criminals and led to the greatest decade of violence since the Civil War. This is not God's way. Rather than restraining their political power Christians and their sympathizers acted as authoritarians seizing the liberty and freedom of their fellow citizens that God gave them to choose how they would live.

Similarly. authoritarians seek to use their power to limit gambling options through zoning regulations. Somehow, they believe that they have a right to prevent people from using their earnings in gaming. The same game played without money is permissible to them but as soon as someone can lose or win money with a game, suddenly the moral, elite authoritarians must take away this option.

Authoritarians are not just those in political office but even worse are those in the community who support the actions of the authoritarians. In recent years, great division occurred in communities between those who supported the power of authoritarians in political office to force people to wear masks and accept vaccines into their bodies and to limit businesses from operating.

It is not that way with God. His greatest desire is that we would choose to do right, to listen to wisdom, to love others. Yet, He is a Father who loves always, teaches, blesses, and hopes that we will choose Him, choose His wisdom, and choose to be like Him. He does not coerce or threaten His children. He does not take away the sources of our desires even if they might be unsafe or destructive. He restrains His awesome power to leave room for us to make our own decisions. He waits patiently for us to learn from our mistakes. He grieves when He sees our suffering from our mistakes and poor choices but does not remove our choices. Instead, he welcomes us back when we are ready to turn away from our bad choices.

GOD'S TOOLS

We have established that God is not an authoritarian. We have established that He values our liberty to choose above all things. This is love modeled by our God and creator.

Persuasion, prayer, love, joy, peace, patience, kindness, goodness, faithfulness, self-control are His tools, given to us for our relationships in this life.

PERSUASION VS FORCE

Of course, the battle is not exclusively in the flesh. It is a spiritual battle that, to be truly effective, must be fought with spiritual weapons. The weapons of the armor of God, the helmet of salvation, the breastplate of righteousness, the shield of faith and the sword of truth. Our weapons also include prayer and fasting, declarations of authority over the environment and spirit world and supernatural power in the Holy Spirit. We must engage the battle while we remain here, and we must understand that we are fighting the enemy of God who wants to strip us of our lives, liberty, and justice.

> *which He brought about in Christ, when He raised Him from the dead and seated Him at His right hand in the heavenly places, far above all rule and authority and power and dominion, and every name that is named, not only in this age but also in the one to come. Ephesians 1:20-21*

and He is the head over all rule and authority;
Colossians 2:10

Satan is the father of authoritarianism. He is the one who comes to steal and kill and destroy, especially liberty. Because liberty is love.

GOD AND PROPERTY RIGHTS

In the earlier chapter, "What is Liberty?", we explored the truth that liberty is not simply the absence of constraint, nor is it merely a political concept. Liberty is sovereignty. It is the God-given authority to govern what has been entrusted to us—our bodies, our minds, our labor, our earnings, and our property. In short, liberty means being free to steward the life and gifts God has given us without coercion.

That definition finds its foundation not in the Enlightenment or in modern constitutions, but in the earliest pages of Scripture.

DOMINION: GOD'S FIRST GIFT OF SOVEREIGNTY

One of the first things God gave to humanity was dominion. Long before the giving of the Law, the establishment of Israel, or even the Fall, God's posture toward humanity was one of delegation and empowerment.

> *"Be fruitful and multiply, and fill the earth, and subdue it; and rule over the fish of the sea and over the birds of the sky and over every living thing that moves on the earth."* —Genesis 1:28

This is not merely a command to populate the earth, but an entrusting of authority. The Hebrew word for "rule" here implies governance, stewardship, and responsibility. God, the Sovereign of the Universe, delegated a portion of His sovereignty to humanity. He gave us the earth not as slaves or tenants but as rulers—under His ultimate authority, but with real responsibility and real liberty.

This concept is revolutionary. It flies in the face of the pagan worldview that viewed humans as playthings of the gods, born to serve the whims of divine rulers. In Scripture, God creates humans in His own image and entrusts them with real agency. That is liberty. That is the foundation of every biblical understanding of rights, ownership, and responsibility.

The Land Promise: A Covenant of Ownership

Nowhere is the principle of God-given sovereignty more clearly illustrated than in the promises made to Abraham.

In Genesis 12, God calls Abram out of Ur and promises him land— not a metaphorical homeland, not just a spiritual promise, but literal land with borders and boundaries:

"To your descendants I will give this land." —Genesis 12:7

This promise was repeated and expanded upon in Genesis 13:

"Now lift up your eyes and look from the place where you are…for all the land which you see, I will give it to you and to your descendants forever."—Genesis 13:14–15

And again, in Genesis 15, with covenantal formality:

"I am the LORD who brought you out of Ur of the Chaldeans, to give you this land to possess it."—Genesis 15:7

And once more in Genesis 17:

"I will give to you and to your descendants after you…all the land of Canaan, for an everlasting possession."—Genesis 17:8

These are not vague blessings. They are legal, covenantal, territorial promises. God was giving Abraham a deed to the land. Though he would live as a sojourner, and though the possession of the land would be delayed for generations, the promise of ownership was immediate, irrevocable, and rooted in divine authority.

The physicality of the promise matters. God was not simply giving Abraham good feelings, or a moral example, or a vision of spiritual destiny. He was giving him land—soil, water, cities, hills, pastures. Liberty includes land. Ownership is part of God's covenantal order.

PRIVATE PROPERTY AND BOUNDARIES

Fast forward several generations. The descendants of Abraham, now the twelve tribes of Israel, stand at the edge of the Promised Land under the leadership of Joshua. The conquest of Canaan is not only a fulfillment of God's promises, but also a reassertion of the principle of liberty through land ownership.

The Book of Joshua outlines, in painstaking detail, the division of the land among the tribes. Joshua sends out men to survey the land. Lots are cast to determine which tribe receives which territory. Borders are drawn. Cities are named.

Why such specificity?

Because liberty is not vague. It is not theoretical. It is measurable, definable, and critically, bounded.

Boundaries are essential to liberty. The dividing lines between one tribe's territory and another's are not merely for administrative ease. They signify ownership. This tribe governs this land. That tribe governs that land. One does not intrude upon the other. Each has sovereignty over what is theirs.

This principle is echoed throughout Scripture. Consider Proverbs 22:28:

> *"Do not move the ancient boundary which your fathers have set."*

Or again in Deuteronomy 19:14:

> *"You shall not move your neighbor's boundary mark, which the ancestors have set in your inheritance."*

In God's law, to violate another's property is to violate that person's liberty.

OWNERSHIP IS NOT A HUMAN CONSTRUCT. IT IS A DIVINE RIGHT ESTABLISHED BY GOD FROM THE VERY BEGINNING.

Private property is not a vice to be managed; it is a virtue to be protected. God's law is full of provisions to prevent theft, fraud, and unjust seizure. Justice in Israel was deeply tied to honoring the boundaries God had ordained.

THE YEAR OF JUBILEE: LIBERTY RESTORED

One of the most remarkable expressions of liberty in the Bible is the institution of the Year of Jubilee, outlined in Leviticus 25. Every fiftieth year, all Israelite land that had been sold or transferred due to debt was to be returned to its original family.

> *"You shall thus consecrate the fiftieth year and proclaim a release through the land to all its*

inhabitants. It shall be a jubilee for you, and each of you shall return to his own property, and each of you shall return to his family."—Leviticus 25:10

This was not socialism. It was not a denial of ownership. In fact, it was the ultimate affirmation of ownership. Land was not to be permanently alienated from families. Temporary sales due to poverty were just that, temporary. The Jubilee ensured that no one would be dispossessed forever. It was a safeguard of liberty, a reset button for economic justice, a divine correction to the inevitable drift of power and wealth toward consolidation.

The Jubilee protected families. It honored inheritance. It maintained liberty through restoration. Even slaves, those who had sold themselves into servitude, were to be released in the Jubilee.

It is difficult to imagine a more comprehensive expression of God's heart for liberty. The Jubilee is not just a quaint Old Testament tradition. It is a theological declaration: people are not property. Land is not infinitely tradeable. Liberty matters more than profit. And God is the ultimate owner who delegates, not hoards.

OWNERSHIP AS SACRED TRUST

Scripture consistently affirms that while God owns all things, He chooses to entrust some of His creation to human beings.

"The earth is the Lord's, and all it contains."— Psalm 24:1

Yet He gives stewardship of specific parts of the earth to specific people. Abraham received a land. The Israelites received territories. Farmers received fields. Shepherds received flocks.

And with that ownership came responsibility. Landowners were commanded to leave gleanings in their fields for the poor (Leviticus

19:9–10). The poor had a right to glean, not to seize, but to access what was left behind by the landowner's intentional generosity.

This strikes a balance between liberty and compassion. Ownership does not nullify community responsibility, **but responsibility never nullifies ownership.**

In God's economy, property is both a right and a trust.

The Sabbath and the Jubilee were economic and spiritual safeguards. Every seventh year was a Sabbath year. Fields lay fallow. Debts were forgiven. The people rested.

In our modern world, rest is often seen as laziness. But in the Bible, rest is liberty. It is a recognition that man is not a machine. It is an act of faith that God will provide. It is a weekly reminder that we are not slaves. We are sons and daughters.

This rhythm of work and rest protected against tyranny—economic, physical, and spiritual. It interrupted cycles of debt and overwork. It prevented perpetual bondage.

In the Sabbath, as in the Jubilee, we see again God's pattern: freedom matters. Restoration is sacred. The land is to be honored, the people to be liberated, the economy to be humanized.

THE DANGER OF FORGETTING LIBERTY

Throughout Israel's history, the erosion of liberty often began with the erosion of property rights and personal responsibility. Kings like Ahab seized land unjustly (1 Kings 21). Wealthy landowners ignored the laws of gleaning. Slaves were held beyond the Jubilee year. Debts were not forgiven.

And with each violation, judgment followed. The prophets cried out against these injustices. Isaiah condemned those who "add house to house and join field to field" (Isaiah 5:8). Micah declared:

> *"They covet fields and then seize them, and houses, and take them away. They rob a man and his house, a man and his inheritance."*—Micah 2:2

These were not merely economic crimes. They were spiritual betrayals.

> *To violate property rights is to violate the image of God in another human being. To steal someone's inheritance is to reject the divine design for liberty.*

JESUS AND THE SPIRIT OF LIBERTY

Jesus did not abolish the principle of ownership or stewardship. In His parables, landowners hire workers, pay wages, distribute inheritance. He affirms the concept of reward for labor and faithfulness (Matthew 25:14–30).

But He also confronts greed. He reminds us that possessions are not ultimate. While we have liberty to own, we are warned not to be owned by our possessions.

"Take care and be on your guard against all covetousness, for one's life does not consist in the abundance of possessions."—Luke 12:15

Jesus' Kingdom respects liberty but it transforms it. In Christ, we are called not just to enjoy liberty, but to use it to love, serve, and restore others. **Liberty becomes a tool of grace.**

From Genesis to Revelation, the story of Scripture affirms that liberty is sacred. It is real. It includes property, boundaries, rest, and responsibility. It is a gift from God—delegated, never revoked.

When we honor ownership, when we steward what is ours, when we rest and restore, we participate in the Spirit of Liberty that God wove into creation itself.

Let us then cherish this gift. Let us teach it to our children. And let us build a society where liberty is not merely preached, but practiced—in the fields we own, the debts we forgive, and the freedom we uphold.

THE KINGDOM ACCORDING TO JESUS

One of the earliest events recorded in the life of Jesus is His temptation in the wilderness, a moment that bears deep theological and philosophical implications for the nature of liberty and God's purposes for humanity. As Matthew recounts:

"Then Jesus was led up by the Spirit into the wilderness to be tempted by the devil. And after He had fasted forty days and forty nights, He then became hungry. And the tempter came and said to Him, 'If You are the Son of God, command that these stones become bread.' But He answered and said, 'It is written, *"Man shall not live on bread alone, but on every word that proceeds out of the mouth of God."'"* (Matthew 4:1-4)

This moment of vulnerability and confrontation sets the tone for understanding God's view of human liberty. Jesus' encounter with the devil is not merely a symbolic event or a distant religious lesson—it is a paradigm of the very structure of human existence under divine liberty.

THE NECESSITY OF TRUE TEMPTATION

Many believers read this passage with the assumption that Jesus, being divine, was incapable of sinning, and thus, the temptation was purely performative. But this is to undermine the gravity of what occurred. Scripture makes clear:

"For we do not have a high priest who cannot sympathize with our weaknesses, but One who has been tempted in all things as we are, yet without sin." (Hebrews 4:15)

Jesus' temptation was real. He was truly hungry. He truly wanted to fulfill His mission as the Son of God. He truly had the power to take the kingdoms of the world by force. Satan did not tempt Jesus with trivialities; he tempted Him with what was deeply desired. Yet, Jesus did not sin.

God did not shield Jesus from temptation. He did not block Satan from approaching Him. He allowed His Son to enter into the wilderness of liberty, that arena where choices must be made, where righteousness must be freely chosen, not imposed.

This temptation account echoes the Garden of Eden. Just as Adam and Eve were presented with a choice, so too was Jesus. In Eden, liberty was misused. In the wilderness, liberty was perfected. Jesus, the Second Adam, shows what true liberty looks like: the power to choose righteousness.

Each temptation Jesus faced corresponds to a core element of human liberty:

1. **Provision** – "Turn these stones into bread." Will you use your power to serve yourself or trust God?

2. **Pride** – "Throw Yourself down; God will save you." Will you manipulate God for your purposes?

3. **Power** – "Worship me, and I'll give you the kingdoms." Will you compromise for immediate gain?

Jesus answered with Scripture, not force

TEMPTATION AS A FEATURE OF LIBERTY

Temptation is not an accident of existence; it is a built-in element of liberty. If there is no real alternative, then there is no real liberty. God does not eliminate temptation from the human experience because to do so would eliminate liberty.

In His prayer, Jesus taught His disciples:

> "Your Kingdom come. Your will be done, on earth as it is in heaven." (Matthew 6:10)

This is not a plea for divine force; it is a request for voluntary alignment. For God's will to be done on earth, people must be free to choose it. And if they are to be free to choose God, they must also be free to reject Him.

God waits for our yes. He never overrides our no.

Jesus further illustrates this principle through parables, particularly the story of the Prodigal Son in Luke 15. The younger son asks for his inheritance, a request both bold and dishonorable. The father gives it to him, knowing the risks. He does not interfere. He allows his son to leave, to sin, to suffer. He watches from a distance.

> "But while he was still a long way off, his father saw him and felt compassion for him, and ran and embraced him." (Luke 15:20)

This is the portrait of God, a father who gives liberty, even when it breaks His heart. The son had to choose to return. The father did not drag him back. **Love does not override liberty.**

Authoritarianism Rejected

Jesus also teaches His disciples to reject authoritarianism:

"You know that the rulers of the Gentiles lord it over them, and their great men exercise authority over them. It is not this way among you..."
(Matthew 20:25-28)

Jesus' Kingdom is a kingdom of servants. Not lords. Not enforcers. Not tyrants.

Even at the cross, Jesus did not call down legions of angels. He submitted. He invited. He forgave. His death was a voluntary gift, not an imposed requirement.

God so loved the world that He gave His Son (John 3:16). But the promise of life is only for "whoever believes." Belief cannot be mandated. It cannot be coerced. It must be chosen.

This is why Jesus describes the way as narrow and the gate as small. Few find it, not because God hides it, but because so many refuse to look.

"Enter through the narrow gate..." (Matthew 7:13-14)

God will not force a single soul into Heaven. Liberty is the foundation of love, and God will never override our freedom to say no.

Liberty Revealed in Christ

The temptation of Jesus, like the story of the Prodigal Son, like the teachings on servanthood, like the cross itself, all point to one staggering truth: God honors human liberty. He respects it even to the point of allowing it to crucify His own Son.

But in the resurrection, Jesus offers not just forgiveness but also restoration. He restores the liberty that was misused in Eden. He invites us back to the garden, not as puppets, but as sons and daughters.

And in this restored liberty, we find the essence of God's Kingdom. Not forced compliance. Not blind obedience. But love, freely chosen.

This is the Spirit of Liberty: the freedom to say yes, the dignity to say no, and the grace to return home when we've gone astray.

THE APOSTLES AND LIBERTY

Liberty and Voluntary Generosity in the Early Church

> *"And all those who had believed were together and had all things in common; and they began selling their property and possessions and were sharing them with all, as anyone might have need." (Acts 2:44–45)*

> *"And the congregation of those who believed were of one heart and soul; and not one of them claimed that anything belonging to him was his own, but all things were common property to them... there was not a needy person among them..." (Acts 4:32–34)*

When the Spirit of God fell upon the people at Pentecost, something extraordinary happened—not only in their hearts, but in their daily lives. It wasn't merely a spiritual revival or a surge of religious enthusiasm. It was a deep transformation that radically reshaped how the early believers viewed their possessions, their neighbors, and the very purpose of life itself.

This radical generosity and shared life were not imposed. There was no command from the Apostles, no formal policy, no communal contract signed or enforced. Instead, this early church exhibited a phenomenon almost foreign to our modern age: voluntary generosity born from liberty and love.

What we see in the early chapters of Acts is not an economic system or a political platform. It is not the forerunner to socialism or communism. It is the Spirit of God, moving freely among believers who had been freed from the bondage of sin, and consequently, from the bondage of self-centeredness.

This transformation wasn't rooted in ideology but in identity. These men and women had encountered the risen Jesus. They had received the Holy Spirit. Their priorities were no longer dictated by status, wealth, or accumulation. They were living under a new reign, a Kingdom not of this world.

Under this Kingdom, generosity was no longer a burden; it was a joy. Possessions were no longer idols or security blankets; they were tools to bless others. And liberty was no longer a license for selfishness but a means for self-giving.

THE DIFFERENCE BETWEEN COERCION AND CONVICTION

It is critical to distinguish between what occurred in Acts and what many propose today in systems of enforced economic equality. In the early church, giving was entirely voluntary. The believers "began selling their property" on their own initiative. The grammar of the passage reveals this as an ongoing, organic process, not a mandate or a requirement.

No Apostle issued a rule requiring the sale of possessions. No one was penalized for keeping their land. The transformation came from within, not from above.

This is a crucial distinction. In God's Kingdom, love is the engine, not legislation. The economy of grace does not operate by decree, but by desire. It is not enforced; it is inspired.

This is why Peter's rebuke of Ananias and Sapphira in Acts 5 is so instructive. When Ananias secretly withholds part of the sale of his property but presents it as if he gave the full amount, Peter confronts him not for keeping the money, but for lying.

> "While it remained unsold, did it not remain your own? And after it was sold, was it not under your control?" (Acts 5:4)

Peter's words affirm the continued existence of private property and personal sovereignty. The issue was deception, not ownership. Ananias was free to keep his land, sell it, or give whatever portion he chose. The sin was hypocrisy—pretending to be more generous than he truly was.

God is not glorified by forced charity. He is glorified when His Spirit moves hearts to give cheerfully and sincerely.

LOVE, LIBERTY, AND OWNERSHIP

Throughout the Bible, ownership is affirmed. From the Garden of Eden, where God gives Adam and Eve dominion, to the laws in Leviticus that protect property boundaries, to Jesus' parables that assume the legitimacy of private possession, the Scripture does not disparage ownership.

Rather, it teaches us how to steward it. Ownership is not abolished in the Kingdom of God; it is transformed. What matters is not the fact that we own, but how we use what we own. Possessions are not evil, but they must not possess us.

Paul reinforces this in his letter to the Corinthians:

> "Each one must do just as he has purposed in his heart, not grudgingly or under compulsion, for God loves a cheerful giver." (2 Corinthians 9:7)

This verse appears in the context of a collection for suffering believers in Jerusalem. Paul encourages generosity but is careful not to mandate it. The goal is not mere funding; it is worship. Giving, like all Kingdom living, must spring from liberty.

This is why socialism, in all its forms, is fundamentally at odds with the values of the Kingdom. It operates on the premise that people cannot be trusted to share freely and thus must be forced to share. But God trusts His people. He trusts that when they are filled with His Spirit, they will act not from fear or guilt, but from love.

It is important to understand that the shared life of the early believers was not a rigid system but a fluid expression of community.

Yes, they had all things in common. But this commonality was relational, not contractual. It arose from being *"of one heart and soul"* (Acts 4:32), not from having signed away their rights. This is why there was no needy person among them, not because the poor were taxed and the rich were punished, but because everyone gave as they were moved.

In many ways, the early church practiced a reversal of Babel. At Babel, people united in pride to build a tower to heaven. In Acts, people united in humility to extend heaven to earth. One was about human power; the other was about divine grace. One demanded conformity; the other invited unity.

THE PERILS OF COERCIVE SYSTEMS

While modern socialist interpretations of Acts 2 and 4 argue that early Christianity was a kind of communalism, this interpretation is not only biblically unfounded but also practically dangerous.

Coercive systems replace God's invitation with human legislation. They trust the state rather than the Spirit. They suppress the freedom to give by eliminating the freedom to withhold. In doing so, they erode the moral value of generosity.

If generosity is no longer a choice, it is no longer a virtue.

Jesus did not come to establish a new economic order. He came to transform hearts. And when hearts are transformed, they act differently with their money, their time, and their lives.

But the order is important: transformation comes first, behavior follows. Coercive systems reverse this: they demand behavior in the hopes it will lead to transformation.

A Church of Liberty Today

The early church's example should challenge modern Christians not to institute policy but to inspire practice. The takeaway is not that we must all sell our homes, but that we must hold nothing back from God.

We must examine our hearts: Are we giving freely or out of obligation? Are we sharing because we're inspired, or because we're pressured? Are we building a community of love or a system of control?

Today, churches that follow this example don't issue tithing mandates or manipulate members with guilt. They teach grace. They point to Jesus. And they trust that a Spirit-filled believer will be more generous than any tax code ever could inspire.

The early chapters of Acts offer us a vision of a church alive with grace and liberty. It is a vision not of enforced equality, but of Spirit-empowered generosity. It is a glimpse of what happens when people are truly free and truly filled with love.

God's Kingdom does not need socialism to feed the poor. It needs saints filled with the Spirit, eager to give. It does not need legislation to enforce justice. It needs liberty to allow love to flourish.

Let us learn from the early church. Let us hold our possessions lightly and our brothers and sisters dearly. Let us give with joy, not obligation. Let us remember that God's Kingdom is built not by compulsion but by compassion, not by coercion but by liberty.

This is the Spirit of Liberty, a Spirit that, when it fills a heart, overflows into the world in love, generosity, and grace.

AUTHORITY VS AUTHORITARIANISM

Even though God is the author of liberty, He is also the author of authority. These are not opposing ideas; they are two dimensions of the same divine character. God created liberty *within* His authority, not apart from it. From before creation, He held all authority within Himself. There was no competing throne, no rival claim. His sovereignty was complete and unchallenged.

Yet, in His wisdom, He chose not to hoard this authority. He delegated it. He gave dominion—limited, but real—into the hands of those He made in His image. This pattern of delegated authority runs from Eden to eternity. It teaches us something essential about both the Kingdom of God and our own responsibility as stewards of liberty.

In Genesis 1:26–28, God gave Adam and Eve dominion over the earth. They were to be fruitful, multiply, fill the earth, subdue it, and rule over all living creatures. This was not a license to exploit but a commission to govern, wisely, faithfully, and in harmony with God.

But this grant of authority came with moral limits. The tree of the knowledge of good and evil was off-limits, not because God feared human empowerment, but because boundaries provide choice. When Adam and Eve disobeyed, they forfeited the authority entrusted to them. In choosing to heed the serpent's voice, they made Satan their master.

From that moment, Satan became "the god of this world" (2 Corinthians 4:4), not by rightful appointment, but by human surrender. He did not steal authority from God. He received it by deception from man.

The fall introduced a perverse distortion into creation. Satan, a created being who had rebelled against God, became the de facto ruler of a fallen world. Jesus Himself refers to him as "the ruler of this world" (John 12:31), indicating that his dominion, while temporary and conditional, was nonetheless real.

This dominion was characterized by oppression, deception, and fear. Authoritarianism, whether in families, nations, or spiritual systems, flows from this polluted source. It is power wielded apart from God, often cloaked in religious or political language. It seeks control without accountability and dominance without justice. But this rule was never meant to last. From the moment of the fall, God set in motion a redemptive plan to reclaim authority through a new Man, Jesus Christ.

JESUS: THE RESTORATION OF ALL AUTHORITY

When Jesus rose from the dead, He made a definitive declaration:

> *"All authority in heaven and on earth has been given to Me." (Matthew 28:18)*

This is not a metaphor. It is a cosmic transfer of power. Jesus, the Second Adam, regained what the first Adam lost. Satan's rule was broken. Death was defeated. The rightful King had returned.

And what does Jesus do with this authority? He delegates it—again. Not to angels, nor to political powers, but to His disciples. He says, *"Go therefore and make disciples of all nations…"* (Matthew 28:19). This is not just a missionary command; it is a Kingdom commission.

Jesus entrusts the work of His Kingdom to His people—not as conquerors, but as ambassadors.

Just as God delegated authority to Adam and Eve to cultivate the earth, Jesus delegates authority to the church to advance His Kingdom. But this authority is not for self-glory. It is for service, proclamation, healing, and truth. It must always be exercised in submission to the King.

GOD HAS ALL AUTHORITY, BUT HE IS NOT AUTHORITARIAN.

This distinction is essential. Authoritarianism, as seen in fallen humans, is power without restraint, command without compassion, control without relationship. It is the default setting of human nature after the fall.

But God's authority is never self-serving. He does not force obedience. He woos it. He does not manipulate loyalty. He earns it by love. This is seen most clearly in the rebellion of Lucifer. God did not strip Lucifer of the ability to rebel. He permitted it. But He did not allow it to stand uncontested.

> *"And the angels who did not keep their own domain, but abandoned their proper abode, He has kept in eternal bonds..." (Jude 1:6)*
>
> *"I saw Satan fall like lightning from heaven." (Luke 10:18)*

Lucifer said in his heart, *"I will ascend...I will raise my throne...I will sit above..."* (Isaiah 14:13), but God cast him down. Even so, God allowed Lucifer's rebellion to run its course through human history—for a time.

Why? Because liberty demands the opportunity to choose—even wrongly. God's authority is so secure that He can permit rebellion without being threatened by it. And because He is just, He judges rebellion in His perfect time.

KORAH'S REBELLION: A CASE STUDY IN USURPED AUTHORITY

Nowhere is the danger of rebellion clearer than in the story of Korah (Numbers 16). Korah and his company challenged Moses and Aaron, claiming that all the people were holy and questioning Moses' leadership.

At first glance, Korah's argument sounds egalitarian, even democratic. *"All the congregation is holy... why do you exalt yourselves?"* But their motives were not purity or justice. They were pride and envy masked in spiritual language.

Moses, the most humble man on earth (Numbers 12:3), did not defend himself. He left the matter to God. And God responded with terrifying clarity: the earth swallowed Korah and his followers, and fire consumed 250 others.

But the people still didn't understand. The very next day, they blamed Moses for the deaths! God's judgment was swift again—a plague broke out, and only the intercession of Aaron stopped it. Nearly 15,000 people died because of one rebellion.

What can we learn? That rebellion against *rightful* authority is not simply a personal disagreement—it is a rejection of God's order. And attempting to operate *within* that order while rejecting its authority is spiritual usurpation.

> *"Rebellion is as the sin of witchcraft, and insubordination is as iniquity and idolatry." (1 Samuel 15:23)*

This is because rebellion and witchcraft both attempt to seize control through illegitimate means. They both reject God's timing, God's placement, and God's boundaries.

HUMAN AUTHORITY IN GOD'S KINGDOM

In the time between Christ's first and second coming, God delegates slices of His authority to humans: to parents, pastors, judges, governors, kings, and other leaders. This delegated authority is always limited, always accountable, and always under the rule of Christ.

"Submit yourselves for the Lord's sake to every human institution..." (1 Peter 2:13)

"Remind them to be subject to rulers, to authorities, to be obedient, to be ready for every good deed." (Titus 3:1)

We are to submit—not because human authority is perfect, but because God is. Submission does not mean silence in the face of injustice, nor does it mean enabling tyranny. But it does mean that we honor the boundaries God has established.

When authorities act *within* their God-ordained boundaries, we are to obey. When they step *outside* those boundaries and command what God forbids, or forbid what God commands, then we must obey God rather than men (Acts 5:29). But even in resistance, we are to remain honorable.

Jesus is not merely a historical figure. He is the reigning King of Kings. He is seated "far above all rule and authority and power and dominion" (Ephesians 1:21). All earthly powers are subject to Him—even those that do not recognize it.

"He is the head over all rule and authority."
(Colossians 2:10)

Every act of human government, every court ruling, every parental command, every church decision will ultimately be weighed against His perfect standard. His throne is above all. His justice is final. His mercy is available.

And Jesus does not rule by coercion. He invites. He teaches. He heals. He speaks. He knocks on the door—not with a battering ram, but with nail-scarred hands.

Those who exercise authority in His name must do likewise.

AUTHORITARIANISM: A CHILDISH WAY OF THINKING

Paul writes in 1 Corinthians 13:11:

"When I was a child, I used to speak like a child, think like a child, reason like a child; when I became a man, I did away with childish things."

Authoritarianism is a childish way of relating to power. It seeks control because it lacks trust. It forces obedience because it cannot inspire it. It punishes disagreement because it fears being questioned.

Mature authority, by contrast, resembles the leadership of Jesus: servant-hearted, truthful, patient, and just. It does not dominate; it disciples. It does not coerce; it compels by love.

It is time for authoritarians—whether in the home, the church, or the state—to grow up and leave childish ways behind.

God never asks us to submit mindlessly. He asks us to discern, to trust, and to obey within the framework of His Word. We are not to rebel just because we dislike authority. Nor are we to tolerate oppression disguised as righteousness.

Jonathan Mayhew, a preacher in the years before the Declaration of Independence drew a distinction in regard to submitting to authority from the Bible. He challenges Romans 13's common interpretation as requiring absolute obedience, even to tyrants:

> *"What unprejudiced man can think that God made ALL to be thus subservient to the lawless pleasure and frenzy of ONE, so that it shall always be a sin to resist him! ... Nothing but the most plain and express revelation from heaven could make a sober impartial man believe such a monstrous, unaccountable doctrine..."*

Mayhew reasons that **the apostle Paul's command to submit** was not intended to justify *blind obedience*, but rather to honor *just authority* that promotes the welfare of society.

> *"The apostle's argument is... for submission to those rulers who exercise their power in a proper manner: And... weak and unconnected... if it be supposed... to tyrannical, oppressive rulers..."*

This is the distinction between Authority and Authoritarian. The latter abuses people and the people cannot be expected to submit to the abuse. The former is the godly Authority who protects the people.

Thomas Jefferson put it this way in the Declaration of Independence,

> *"That whenever any Form of Government becomes destructive of these ends, it is the Right of the People to alter or to abolish it,... But when a long train of abuses and usurpations, pursuing*

invariably the same Object evinces a design to reduce them under absolute Despotism, it is their right, it is their duty, to throw off such Government, and to provide new Guards for their future security."

Godly authority is a gift, not a weapon. It brings order, safety, growth, and justice. But it must remain within its proper bounds.

When leaders overreach, God may remove them. When people rebel without cause, they may reap judgment. But when both leader and follower operate under Christ, the result is peace, fruitfulness, and joy.

FROM LIBERTY TO AUTHORITARIANISM

Throughout Christian history, the tension between liberty and authority has persisted as one of its most enduring and divisive themes. The teachings of Jesus emphasized servant leadership, humility, and personal transformation, yet as the Church grew from a persecuted minority to a dominant institution, it frequently succumbed to authoritarian impulses. From imperial alliances to theocratic structures, inquisitions to contemporary cults, authoritarianism has periodically distorted the gospel's liberating message into tools for control.

THE EARLY CHURCH: SEEDS OF STRUCTURE AND CONTROL

In its earliest phase, the Christian community operated informally and communally. Early texts like Acts 2 describe believers sharing all things in common, with leadership exercised by apostles who led through example and exhortation rather than compulsion. However, as Christianity expanded, organizational necessities emerged. Bishops, presbyters, and deacons arose to maintain doctrinal unity and communal care.

The letters of Ignatius of Antioch (early 2nd century) offer an early window into this growing emphasis on centralized ecclesiastical authority. He stressed obedience to bishops as a safeguard against heresy. Though rooted in a desire to preserve the faith, this emerging hierarchical structure laid the groundwork for later authoritarian patterns, as the bishop increasingly became not merely a servant leader but a singular voice of control.

By the time of Cyprian of Carthage (3rd century), the concept of *episcopal authority* had solidified, justifying centralized power in the Church as divinely ordained. Cyprian's famous dictum, *"He cannot have God for his Father who has not the Church for his mother"*, elevated ecclesiastical authority nearly to the level of salvation itself.

CONSTANTINE AND THE RISE OF CHRISTENDOM

The most dramatic shift came in the 4th century when Emperor Constantine legalized Christianity (Edict of Milan, 313 AD) and began aligning the Church with the Roman state. The Council of Nicaea (325 AD), while theologically crucial, also marked the first instance of an emperor calling and presiding over a Church council. Christianity was on the path to becoming the state religion.

The newfound power granted to the Church came at a price. Church leaders became entangled with imperial politics, and doctrinal enforcement began to take on state-like mechanisms. Heretics were no longer simply excommunicated. They were exiled, imprisoned, or even executed.

By the late 4th century, under Emperor Theodosius I, Christianity had become the Roman Empire's official religion. Pagan temples were shuttered. Deviant sects were outlawed. The line between state and Church blurred dramatically, ushering in centuries of authoritarian entwinement.

THE CHURCH HAD GONE FROM PERSECUTED TO PERSECUTOR.

THE MEDIEVAL CHURCH: THE PAPACY AND THE INQUISITION

The medieval Church represents one of the clearest examples of authoritarianism in Christian history. The Papacy gradually amassed not only spiritual authority but political power, often surpassing that of kings. Popes crowned emperors, settled disputes between monarchs, and wielded the weapon of excommunication to enforce submission.

The 11th-century Investiture Controversy between Pope Gregory VII and Emperor Henry IV illustrates how the papacy asserted dominance over secular rulers. Gregory's *Dictatus Papae* declared that the pope could depose emperors—a claim of divine authority over all earthly powers.

The notion that the Pope held the "keys to the kingdom" morphed from spiritual stewardship to political absolutism. Dissent, even when theological, became treasonous. The Church institutionalized mechanisms of control and surveillance that mirrored the authoritarian state.

THE INQUISITION

Perhaps the most infamous symbol of ecclesiastical authoritarianism is the Inquisition. Initiated in the 12th century, with its most powerful arm being the Spanish Inquisition (established 1478), the Church created a formal apparatus to detect, try, and punish heresy.

These tribunals used coercive interrogations, forced confessions, and public executions to maintain orthodoxy. Not only did this violate the core Christian teachings of mercy and free will, but it also created a climate of fear and intellectual stagnation. While some defenders argue the Inquisition was less brutal than portrayed, its institutionalization of religious terror cannot be denied.

THE PROTESTANT REFORMATION AND AUTHORITARIAN RESPONSES

The Reformation of the 16th century arose partly in protest against the authoritarianism of the Roman Church. Reformers like Martin Luther, John Calvin, and Ulrich Zwingli called for a return to Scripture and a rejection of papal absolutism.

Yet the Reformation did not always result in greater liberty. In some cases, it exchanged one form of authoritarianism for another.

LUTHER AND STATE CHURCH ALLIANCES

Though Luther championed liberty of conscience early on, he later supported harsh suppression of dissenters like the Anabaptists. He also sanctioned the princes' violent response to the Peasants' Revolt (1525), urging obedience to secular rulers even when they acted unjustly. This entangled Lutheranism with state power, creating new Church-state authoritarian hybrids in Protestant lands.

CALVIN'S GENEVA

John Calvin's Geneva presents another paradox. A theocracy in form, Geneva enforced moral conformity through Church courts, exiled or executed heretics like Michael Servetus, and punished non-attendance at worship. Though grounded in a desire for a godly society, the fusion of theology and civil enforcement became a template for later forms of spiritual authoritarianism cloaked in reformist ideals. Speaking out against Calvin could lead to death by drowning. They sought to bring the Kingdom of God on earth through force, threats and intimidation.

THE PILGRIMS

The Pilgrims who sailed on the *Mayflower* in 1620 were part of a Separatist movement that broke away from the Church of England. They believed that the Church was too corrupt to reform from within and sought to practice their faith freely. In England, Separatists faced persecution under laws that made attendance at Anglican services mandatory. Their leaders were arrested, fined, or harassed. To escape this religious authoritarianism, many of them fled first to the Netherlands (Leiden), where there was more religious tolerance.

Although the Dutch allowed them to worship freely, the Pilgrims felt they were losing their English identity and feared that their children were assimilating into Dutch culture. They also wanted to evangelize and build a covenant community according to their own values. So they arranged to sail to the New World.

Upon arrival, the Pilgrims established Plymouth Colony. Their guiding vision was a *covenant community* governed by biblical principles. While they had fled religious coercion in England, they did not believe in a pluralistic society where all faiths or beliefs should coexist equally.

Instead, they created a theocratic social order. Church membership was often tied to political participation. Dissent from core beliefs or church authority could be punished harshly—

sometimes by exile, public shaming, or imprisonment. Over time, especially in Massachusetts Bay Colony (established in 1630 by the Puritans, who were more numerous and more rigid), this impulse toward religious conformity deepened.

EXAMPLES OF AUTHORITARIANISM

Roger Williams (founder of Rhode Island) was banished from Massachusetts Bay Colony for advocating religious liberty and separation of church and state.

Anne Hutchinson was also exiled for holding private Bible studies and challenging male leadership.

Laws mandated church attendance, and blasphemy or heresy could be criminal offenses.

In some cases, the colonies used corporal punishment or execution for religious crimes (e.g., Quakers being hanged for returning after banishment).

The Pilgrims and their Puritan cousins sought to escape religious authoritarianism but ended up creating communities with their own strong religious controls. To them, liberty meant *freedom to build a godly community their way*, not *freedom for everyone to believe differently*. In this sense, they replaced one form of authoritarianism with another—one that aligned with their particular interpretation of Scripture.

Their story remains a powerful reminder that the line between protecting religious liberty and enforcing religious conformity can be perilously thin.

REVIVALISM AND THE AUTHORITARIAN TURN TOWARD MORAL LEGISLATION IN THE

UNITED STATES

The American religious landscape, particularly in the 18th and 19th centuries, was profoundly shaped by revivalism. The First Great Awakening (1730s–40s) and especially the Second Great Awakening (early 1800s) stirred millions into a vibrant and emotional form of personal faith. These revivals emphasized individual conversion, repentance, and *personal holiness*—a transformed life evidenced by moral behavior.

This sincere focus on sanctification, however, often carried an unintended consequence: the belief that if personal holiness was good for the individual, it should be legislated for the whole nation. The result was a shift from inward transformation to outward enforcement—an attempt to mold American society through law, policy, and even coercion.

1. The Holiness and Temperance Movements

Following the Second Great Awakening, the *Holiness Movement*— an outgrowth of Methodism—emphasized entire sanctification and the pursuit of a sinless life. This movement soon merged with the *Temperance Movement*, which sought to eradicate the societal evil of alcohol consumption.

While temperance began as a moral and spiritual call to sobriety, it evolved into a legal campaign. Advocates lobbied for local and national laws banning alcohol, culminating in the 18th Amendment (Prohibition, 1920–1933). The enforcement of temperance through federal law marked one of the clearest examples of revivalist spirituality turning to legal authoritarianism.

Ironically, while revivalism had celebrated individual liberty in coming to Christ, its legacy helped produce one of the most restrictive periods in American legal history highlighting how even well-intentioned moral reform can lead to authoritarian overreach when tied to the state.

2. Sabbatarian Laws and Blue Laws

In the same spirit, religious groups pressured lawmakers to enact *blue laws*, which enforced Sabbath observance by banning certain activities on Sundays—such as business operations, alcohol sales, and public entertainment. Though rooted in the biblical idea of rest, these laws imposed sectarian views of Sabbath observance on a pluralistic public.

While many blue laws have since been repealed, they represented a religiously-motivated use of government power to mandate religious behavior, an authoritarian impulse cloaked in the language of morality and order.

While these efforts were driven by genuine concern for the nation's spiritual health, they often took on authoritarian tones. Rather than evangelizing hearts, the focus turned to legislating behavior and punishing transgressions of Christian norms. In this context, Christian engagement with politics drifted from prophetic witness to political power brokerage.

This shift from persuasion to coercion undercut the Church's witness. Many Americans began to associate Christianity not with compassion, humility, or service—but with cultural dominance and control.

THE SHEPHERDING MOVEMENT (1970s– 1980s)

One of the most documented authoritarian experiments in modern evangelicalism was the Shepherding Movement, also known as the Discipleship Movement. Originating in the charismatic revival of the 1970s, it was spearheaded by five prominent leaders: Don

Basham, Bob Mumford, Derek Prince, Charles Simpson, and Ern Baxter—sometimes called the "Fort Lauderdale Five."

The movement emphasized accountability, submission to spiritual authority, and mentoring relationships. In theory, this addressed real concerns about spiritual growth and community. In practice, it degenerated into rigid hierarchies that fostered abuse.

Members were required to submit to a "shepherd" who had the authority to direct their personal, financial, and even marital decisions. These leaders claimed spiritual discernment over individuals' lives, discouraging independent thought or disagreement as rebellion against God's order.

The concept of *covering*, a supposed spiritual protection provided by one's shepherd, was used to bind individuals to hierarchical loyalty, despite growing concerns over manipulation.

By the 1980s, backlash grew. Victims reported emotional and spiritual abuse, and prominent Christian leaders criticized the movement for cult-like tendencies. Eventually, some of the original founders publicly repented. Bob Mumford, for example, issued a formal apology in 1989, admitting the movement had become oppressive and harmful.

AUTHORITARIAN CULTS AND NEW RELIGIOUS MOVEMENTS

Authoritarianism in the church has also emerged in extreme and often tragic forms in cults and high-control groups. Though the term "cult" can be pejorative, it broadly refers to groups that exert excessive control over members' lives, often centered around a single charismatic leader who claims divine authority.

Jim Jones began as a Disciples of Christ pastor who advocated for racial integration and social justice. However, he devolved into a messianic figure who demanded absolute loyalty. His Peoples Temple ended in the 1978 Jonestown massacre in Guyana, where over 900 people died in a mass murder-suicide. Jones's descent into paranoia and control is a sobering warning about unchecked religious authority.

David Koresh led a sectarian offshoot of Seventh-Day Adventism. Styling himself as the Lamb of God, Koresh controlled every aspect of his followers' lives, including marriages and sexual relations. The 1993 siege in Waco, Texas, ended in tragedy, with over 70 people dead after a botched federal raid. Though the federal actions were controversial, Koresh's authoritarian leadership and spiritual manipulation were undeniable.

Other groups such as the Church of Scientology (though not traditionally Christian), the International Churches of Christ (which has reformed in many areas), and smaller independent churches continue to demonstrate how spiritual language can be twisted into psychological control. Common traits include isolation from outside influence, rigid authority structures, financial exploitation, and discouragement of critical thinking.

THEOLOGICAL JUSTIFICATIONS FOR AUTHORITARIANISM

Throughout history, authoritarian leaders in the Church have drawn on Scripture to justify control. Romans 13 is perhaps the most cited passage: *"Let every person be subject to the governing authorities..."* While intended to encourage respect for civil order, it has been used to justify compliance with tyranny.

Similarly, the biblical concept of *submission* (e.g., Ephesians 5:21) has often been weaponized to demand unquestioning loyalty to pastors, husbands, or leaders, rather than mutual humility under Christ.

One of the most dangerous justifications has been the claim of *divine anointing*—that certain leaders possess a unique authority from God and should not be "touched" or questioned, lest one incur divine wrath (a misapplication of 1 Chronicles 16:22).

A CALL TO SERVANT LEADERSHIP AND LIBERTY

The New Testament consistently models leadership as service. Jesus said, *"The greatest among you must be your servant"* (Matthew 23:11) and warned against lording over others,

> *You know that those who are recognized as rulers of the Gentiles lord it over them; and their great men exercise authority over them. But it is not this way among you, but whoever wishes to become great among you shall be your servant and whoever wishes to be first among you shall be slave of all. For even the Son of Man did not come to be served, but to serve, and to give His life a ransom for many.*

- Mark 10:42-45

Peter wrote of leading by example, not compulsion

> *Therefore, I exhort the elders among you, as your fellow elder and witness of the sufferings of Christ, and a partaker also of the glory that is to be revealed, shepherd the flock of God among you, exercising oversight not under compulsion, but*

voluntarily, according to the will of God; and not for sordid gain, but with eagerness; nor yet as lording it over those allotted to your charge, but proving to be examples to the flock. - 1 Peter 5:1-3

True godly authority flows from humility, not hierarchy.

Vigilance is needed. While leadership in a church has responsibility for the church and must protect the sheep, authoritarianism often masquerades as order, loyalty, or vision. Liberty in Christ means freedom not only from sin but also from oppressive human control. The Church must continually reform itself around Christ's example, not of power, but of sacrificial love.

The story of the Church is filled with both profound beauty and heartbreaking abuses of power. Authoritarianism, while never the gospel's intent, has haunted its institutions from the imperial thrones of Constantine to the charismatic pulpits of the 20th century.

By reflecting honestly on this history, the Church can move forward, not by abandoning authority, but by reforming it. Authority in the Christian sense is never about domination but stewardship, never about control but empowerment.

In every generation, the Church must choose again: will it reflect the crucified Savior who stooped to wash feet, or the rulers of this world who grasp for power? The Spirit of liberty, not coercion, is the true mark of the Kingdom of God.

LIBERTY AND CONSENT

A few years ago, during the trial of Henry Weinstein the #MeToo move grew up as more women came forward claiming that they too were assaulted by Weinstein. Again, during the hearings for confirmation of Justice Kavanaugh to the Supreme Court, the #MeToo movement grew in sympathy with the woman Kavanaugh was accused of assaulting back in college. It came about that these accusations were false, but it inspired more women to come forward across the board.

The #MeToo movement brought the idea of consent to the foreground of public discourse in the recent past. Lunatic activists and opportunists aside, millions of American women have a legitimate grievance that men are not respecting their "no". Millions of men are violating the consent of women, applying force and coercion to overcome the resistance of women. The only right and proper rule is that men should NEVER touch a woman without absolute and unequivocal consent from each woman they meet. This applies to women we are married to, in a relationship with, women we are only acquainted with and women that we don't even know. This means that a woman who is intoxicated cannot give consent. If she cannot drive, she cannot consent to sex. If she consents to kissing, she still has not given consent to more. Period.

The #MeToo movement has done us all a great service in bringing the issue of consent into our conversations. What they have not realized is that they have exposed the problem with consent across our society and the world. Consider that religions in many parts of the world and even in this land we call free do not see consent as an important feature of their faith. Many Muslims in the world apply force and violence both against those who leave their faith and against those who do not convert and conform to their faith. They even apply force against members of their own community and family for violations of their faith. Other faiths like Catholicism and Judaism often apply social consequences as a tool to coerce or override consent against those who leave their faith. They do not respect consent.

What if you come across a diary or journal that is not your own? Should you read it even though the owner has not consented? If it is your spouse's journal, do you have a right to read it without consent? This is the same issue as noted above with assault. You may or may not know whose journal it is but you know that it is not yours. You may be completely in private with no prospect of discovery. Do you have a right to read it without consent? The question should arise whether you respect the other person's right to their personal sovereignty. If you do not own it then you must gain consent to read it.

Americans claim that our government governs at the consent of the governed. However, this is not true. Consider that at all times the majority rules over the minority. The minority has not consented. This was supposed to be prevented by our government structure as a Republic. The truth is that our government and elections process function in nearly every way as a pure democracy. The American electorate is very nearly split 50-50 about how we are governed meaning that at all times a minority of 49% are ruled over by the majority who enforce their governance values on the minority. The minority has been stripped of their consent. This is just the same as a man forcing his desires upon a woman, overriding her consent by sheer strength and power.

Some have said that simply living in the US under our current governmental system is implicit consent to be governed in this way.

However, that is the same as saying that women who dress in a certain way or drink too much or flirt too much or walk alone at night are automatically giving consent to be abused.

Many said during the faux pandemic that government should force people to wear a mask or get a vaccination. This is, again, no different than assaulting a woman. That is, the feelings of insecurity lead people to override other people's consent. They are stripping others of their sovereignty over their bodies.

In America, we claim to be the "land of the free". How can we be free when our consent is overridden by others? If we are not secure in our bodies from our consent being stolen, how can we be free? If we are not secure in the labor of our bodies from our consent being overridden, how can we be free? If we are not secure in our earnings of our labor, from our consent being stolen how can we be free? If we are not secure in our property purchased with our earnings, from our consent being taken by the majority how can we be free?

This is most revealed in taxation. As citizens we vote on whether we should collect taxes. Consider that taxation, by definition, is force. Taxation is theft because it overrides consent at the point of force for non-compliance. Some people say that taxation is necessary because we cannot allow anyone to opt out of paying. By definition, this is force. If an idea for spending is good enough people will contribute voluntarily. Only bad ideas need taxation. Or more specifically, fears that ideas are not good enough, or popular enough, need taxation to override consent. Many people cannot imagine a world without taxation because they focus strictly on the spending side of the ledger. They cannot imagine that people would voluntarily pay for roads or police or schools, etc. Since they don't believe in the voluntary, they believe that force is necessary and justified because the spending side is so compelling in their own mind. Yet the truth is this. How someone spends or contributes their own money is a true reflection of how people feel about public policy and governance.

Liberty demands consent.

Given that we have established that liberty applies to external constraints or coercions by others we need to develop a baseline against which to measure liberty and what liberty is not.

Sheffield Resolves produced by the town of Sheffield, MA in 1773 states this baseline well in its first resolution:

> Mankind in a state of nature are equal, free, and independent of each other, and have a right to the undisturbed enjoyment of their lives, their liberty and property,

Thomas Jefferson paraphrased this in the Declaration of Independence as the inalienable rights from our creator as "Life, liberty, and the pursuit of happiness". Unfortunately, his earlier draft of "life, liberty and property" was revised, making the statement vague and weak.

John Locke put it this way regarding property:

> "Through the Earth, and all inferior creatures, be common to all men, yet every man has a property in his own person. This, nobody has any right to but himself. The labor of his body and the work of his hands, we may say, are properly his. "

Locke believed that even before entering into a social contract people were naturally moral. This Law of Nature came from God and demanded that each person do no harm to others in regard to their life, liberty, and possessions. The state of nature is the state of liberty where everyone pursues their own interests without interference. The only limit is the moral boundary of not harming others.

Locke wrote that in addition to the private property of a man's own body, private property is created when a man's labor is added to raw materials. If a man were to labor to cultivate land to produce food for himself and family or cut wood to build a house, he has a moral right to that land as his own property. The Law of Nature would also prohibit one man from taking more land than he could use leaving others without any opportunity to apply their labor to the land for their own property.

"Every man did what was right in his own eyes." Judges 17:6 and 21:25.

This is God's plan for humanity. It was God's "natural", designed condition for humanity. God values liberty so highly, that He put the tree of the knowledge of good and evil into the garden telling Adam and Eve not to eat from it. God risked His entire creation on the choices of these two people. There can be no greater illustration of how God feels about liberty.

This God-designed liberty was the condition of Adam and Eve, Abraham, Isaac, Jacob. Even after God gave the laws to Moses, it was largely up to men to choose to obey. There is no record of any enforcement except for offense against others which was taken before a judge. The only accountability otherwise was to God and conscience. When the people sought to have a King rule over them, they rejected God's plan and design.

> The LORD said to Samuel, "Listen to the voice of the people in regard to all that they say to you, for they have not rejected you, but they have rejected Me from being king over them. - 1 Samuel 8:7

The word we are talking about here as our baseline is SOVEREIGNTY. That is, individual sovereignty over our bodies, our labor, our earnings or fruit of our labor and our property without constraint or coercion by others. This is simple, pure liberty. The right to say "NO".

SOCIAL CONTRACT

In a nutshell, the theory of a social contract tells us that individuals in their natural condition of liberty and sovereignty might agree to surrender some of their liberties and sovereignty in exchange for provisions and activities that a society and government may be able to do better, such as defense, courts (dispute resolution), etc.

In the natural condition of liberty, authoritarians may arise and seek to control others through force. This may be in the form of gangs or marauders. Individuals may join together in a social contract for mutual/common defense against such marauders. However, there are often too few boundaries to such a social contract. They invariably expand, increasing forced cooperation regarding many perceived needs like food, shelter, education, healthcare, law enforcement, and more. It becomes a blank check on which the community draws. The sovereignty of the individual over their bodies, labor, earnings, and property dissolves in favor of the "good of the community". Early on, stoking fears of the unknown is often used by progressives and authoritarians in the community to gain compliance. Later, actual force and violence is used against those who will not comply. Lastly, authority and power are consolidated for the final conformity.

This is all illustrated by the evolution of the US. As we know, the US started out as a collection of colonies under the sovereignty of the Monarchy of Britain. Under British common law which was a quasi "social contract" evolved in various forms from the Magna Carta in 1215, the Crown had responsibilities to protect their subjects, and the subjects had a responsibility to obey the Crown. Disputes of this were to be resolved in the Parliament. However, the Parliament sided with the Crown in the cases of abuse of the colonists. The social contract was broken.

During the ensuing war the states formed a social contract called the "Articles of Confederation". This was designed to gain agreement for all colonies to contribute funds and soldiers for the war as well as provide for a single Congress to conduct foreign affairs, a postal service, coin money and serve as court of last resort on disputes between the states.

However, there was no option for enforcement if states did not uphold their commitments. Remember that this was a voluntary agreement. This was the first crack in the liberty of the new states. This was followed by a Constitution in 1787 which was expressly intended to ensure compliance from the states. Another crack in the liberty of the states and their citizens. Some components of the Constitution such as the 10th amendment would seem to protect the states as sovereign of matters within their boundaries but that too faded into oblivion by the end of the civil war. The greatest flaw in the US Constitution is the lack of a path to legal secession. President Lincoln made it clear that he did not care if any slaves were freed as long as he could keep any states from leaving the union.

> *"My paramount object in this struggle is to save the Union, and it is not either to save or destroy slavery. If I could save the Union without freeing any slave, I would do it"*
>
> -Lincoln wrote to Horace Greeley on Aug. 22, 1862

The federal govt had finally gained supreme power over all matters within its borders including all matters within states. (See 13th, 14th, and 15th amendments.) Liberty was gone. Any sense of choice is only a matter that the government has allowed it and could easily disallow it in the future all by force. For such liberty of choice, we must pay tribute to the central govt in the form of taxation. Still, the govt takes away choices regularly.

In our modern world we have organizations such as NATO which is the functional equivalent to the Articles of Confederation. Members often don't keep up their commitments and there is no enforcement mechanism. Even if a member nation is in arrears the other members will come to their aid. Individual nations retain their sovereignty.

We also have seen the formation of the European Union where member nations surrendered their sovereignty to a higher level central govt. Each member nation must obey the laws and authority of the new govt. This was a huge mistake similar to the mistake of the 13 sovereign states that were independent and at liberty to choose for themselves. Nevertheless, the EU Constitution provided a path to legal secession which the people of Britain chose.

The bottom line is that a social contract MUST ALWAYS provide a legal path of exit and to nullify rules of the community.

Liberty is God's idea. He does not override consent.

GOD AND GOVERNMENT

God created humans with the intention that they would live without external laws. The spirit of love lived within them. In love they would not harm others. No murder, assault or theft. Only when the divine, Holy Spirit left them did their hearts become corrupt, selfish, and evil.

External laws are ineffective. Murder still happens frequently. Assault and theft likewise continue, mostly unabated. The heart of humans is evil continually. The Apostle Paul makes the case for this in Romans. This describes humans in their natural condition without the Spirit of God in them.

> *THERE IS NONE RIGHTEOUS, NOT EVEN ONE;*
> *THERE IS NONE WHO UNDERSTANDS,*
> *THERE IS NONE WHO SEEKS FOR GOD;*
> *ALL HAVE TURNED ASIDE, TOGETHER THEY HAVE BECOME USELESS;*
> *THERE IS NONE WHO DOES GOOD,*
> *THERE IS NOT EVEN ONE.*
> *THEIR THROAT IS AN OPEN GRAVE,*
> *WITH THEIR TONGUES THEY KEEP DECEIVING,*
> *THE POISON OF ASPS IS UNDER THEIR LIPS*
> *WHOSE MOUTH IS FULL OF CURSING AND BITTERNESS*
> *THEIR FEET ARE SWIFT TO SHED BLOOD,*
> *DESTRUCTION AND MISERY ARE IN THEIR PATHS,*
> *AND THE PATH OF PEACE THEY HAVE NOT KNOWN.*
> *THERE IS NO FEAR OF GOD BEFORE THEIR EYES.*

-Romans 3:10-18; Ps 14:1-3;5:9

And yet God promises a path to righteousness

He gives His law to the people of Israel knowing ahead of time that they will fail to keep it. That law is a tutor to teach them of their need for the Messiah, for forgiveness, and for His Spirit to dwell in them.

> *But before faith came, we were kept in custody under the law, being shut up to the faith which was later to be revealed.   Therefore, the Law has become our tutor to lead us to Christ, so that we may be justified by faith.*
>
> -Galatians 3:23-24
>
> *But this is the covenant which I will make with the house of Israel after those days," declares the LORD, "**I will put My law within them and on their heart** I will write it; and I will be their God, and they shall be My people.*
>
> - Jeremiah 31:33

Nevertheless, God's plan was that the people would obey His laws voluntarily. They would have the liberty to refuse. In the giving of the law to the people of Israel, there is no enforcement beyond civil disputes that came before judges. *"Every man did what was right in his own eyes."* -Judges 17:6; 21:25

God is opposed to human authoritarians, yet He gives people over to what they want. He does not condone authoritarians but warns the people of the consequences of their choices.

> *This will be the procedure of the king who will reign over you: he will take your sons and place them for himself in his chariots and among his horsemen*

and they will run before his chariots.[2] He will appoint for himself commanders of thousands and of fifties, and some to do his plowing and to reap his harvest and to make his weapons of war and equipment for his chariots. He will also take your daughters for perfumers and cooks and bakers. He will take the best of your fields and your vineyards and your olive groves and give them to his servants. He will take a tenth of your seed and of your vineyards and give to his officers and to his servants. He will also take your male servants and your female servants and your best young men and your donkeys and use them for his work. He will take a tenth of your flocks, and you yourselves will become his servants. Then you will cry out in that day because of your king whom you have chosen for yourselves, but the LORD will not answer you in that day." -1 Samuel 8:11-18

After several generations of Kings, both the northern and southern Kingdoms of Israel were sent into captivity by God's hand to teach them the consequences of disobeying His laws. After 70 years the southern tribes returned to the land of Israel but they were changed. They committed themselves to fully obey God's laws. However, authoritarians among them devised a plan such that they passed laws of their own with the intent of preventing anyone from breaking God's laws. For example, God's law of not working on the sabbath, became a collection of human laws determining what was work and what would violate God's law. They determined how many steps a person may walk without violating the law. They used these laws to accuse Jesus of working on the sabbath. They heaped great burdens on the people.

The scribes and the Pharisees have seated themselves in the chair of Moses; [3] therefore all that they tell you, do and observe, but do not do according to their deeds; for they say things and do not do them. [4] They tie up heavy burdens and lay them on men's shoulders, but they themselves are unwilling to move them with so much as a finger. -Matthew 23:2-4

Authoritarians have continued in this pattern up to this day, seeking to heap burdens on people to prevent them from breaking the cardinal laws. They seek to ban guns in order to prevent murder. They seek to ban alcohol to prevent domestic abuse. This was not God's plan or design.

It is among the most important laws of God that men and women must be free to choose.

KINGS AND CONSTITUTIONS

For the ages since Jesus, men have claimed a divine mandate for their rule including a divine status that made them better than the people they ruled over. The reformation, beginning around 1512, followed by the enlightenment, began changing that. Treaties like the Magna Carta, began tearing down this idea of divine nature and authority. The protestant movement tore down the idea that the Pontiff of the Catholic church had exclusive authority from God to rule over people. This began the ideal that all men are created equal and have a right to choose their government and laws.

The US Constitution enshrined these values in governing documents. However. President John Adams declared. "Our Constitution was made only for a moral and religious people. It is wholly inadequate to the government of any other." The flaw here is the belief that all people of the new Republic will be of such character. This was certainly naïve and short-sighted. If this was truly the belief of the representatives to the Constitutional

Convention, then we must suggest that they also were naïve and short-sighted. If the Constitution is truly "inadequate" for the government of anyone who is not primarily moral and religious, then what shall we say about that? In our time, we have returned to a time when the majority of people do not have the Spirit of the Lord in their hearts as spoken of by Jeremiah. Therefore, the external laws have needed to multiply in futility. This has led to the gross increase in government, fear, and calls for greater authoritarian rule.

Clearly, the abuses of human government are not new in our age. Human Government has always been corrupt, abusive and murderous in every age and every locale. The hearts of humans are corrupt as described by Paul in Romans. How can any then be allowed to govern others?   Yet, authoritarians among the population far outnumber libertarians. The people of America no longer value liberty. America may have been "conceived in liberty" but liberty was quickly "stillborn" in the face of authoritarianism.

Almost immediately after the Constitution was ratified we have this from Thomas Paine, in his book The Rights of Man, 1791

> We still find the greedy hand of government thrusting itself into every corner and crevice of industry and grasping at the spoil of the multitude. Invention is continually exercised to furnish new pretenses for revenue and taxation. It watches prosperity as its prey and permits none to escape without a tribute.

Frederic Bastiat, in his small book, The Law, 1850 explained liberty and laws this way.

> Life, liberty, and property do not exist because men have made laws. On the contrary, it was the fact that life, liberty, and property existed

beforehand that caused men to make laws in the first place."

Frederic Bastiat, <u>The Law,</u> 1850

The law and, in its wake, all the collective forces of the nation, not only have diverted from its proper direction but made to pursue the one entirely contrary! The law became the tool of every kind of avarice, instead of being its check! The law is guilty of that very iniquity which it was its mission to punish! Truly, this is a serious fact. Frederic Bastiat, <u>The Law,</u> 1850

Government exists to protect us from each other. Where government has gone beyond its limits is in deciding to protect us from ourselves. — Ronald Reagan

"The more corrupt the state, the more numerous the laws." — Tacitus

The federal code has made everything a crime. Politicians and bureaucrats in the role of lawmakers have made everyone a criminal and stomped out liberty everywhere it can be found.

Ayn Rand puts it this way in the mouth of her character Henry Reardon in <u>Atlas Shrugged</u>

"Did you really think we want those laws observed?" said Dr. Ferris. "We want them to be broken. You'd better get it straight that it's not a bunch of boy scouts you're up against... We're after power and we mean it... There's no way to rule innocent men. The only power any government has is the power to crack down on criminals. Well, when there aren't enough

criminals one makes them. One declares so many things to be a crime that it becomes impossible for men to live without breaking laws. Who wants a nation of law-abiding citizens? What's there in that for anyone? But just pass the kind of laws that can neither be observed nor enforced or objectively interpreted – and you create a nation of law-breakers – and then you cash in on guilt. Now that's the system, Mr. Reardon, that's the game, and once you understand it, you'll be much easier to deal with."

THEN HOW IS THE CONSTITUTION TO GOVERN?

We must recognize that only 3 laws are truly necessary: Those against murder, assault, theft.

Instead, we get these:

Civil Asset Forfeiture, money laundering, drug enforcement, Prohibition, licensing, zoning, and taxes.

Our liberty loving and people loving God did not design His people to live this way.

ROMANS 13

Every person is to be in subjection to the governing authorities. For there is no authority except from God, and those which exist are established by God. Therefore whoever resists authority has opposed the ordinance of God; and they who have opposed will receive condemnation upon themselves. For rulers are not a cause of fear for good behavior, but for evil. Do you want to have no fear of authority? Do what is good and you will have praise from the same; for it is a minister of God to you for good. But if you do what is evil, be afraid; for it does not bear the sword for nothing; for it is a minister of God, an avenger who brings wrath on the one who practices evil. Therefore it is necessary to be in subjection, not only because of wrath, but also for conscience' sake. For because of this you also pay taxes, for rulers are servants of God, devoting themselves to this very thing. Render to all what is due them: tax to whom tax is due; custom to whom custom; fear to whom fear; honor to whom honor.

Owe nothing to anyone except to love one another; for he who loves his neighbor has fulfilled the law. For this, "YOU SHALL NOT COMMIT ADULTERY, YOU SHALL NOT MURDER, YOU SHALL NOT STEAL, YOU SHALL NOT COVET," and if there is any other commandment, it is summed up in this saying, "YOU SHALL LOVE YOUR NEIGHBOR AS YOURSELF." Love does no wrong to a neighbor; therefore, love is the fulfillment of the law.

Romans 13:1-10

We have learned so far that God is the author of liberty. He prizes liberty for us higher than all, so much so because He risked his whole creation on it and allowed people to suffer death, spiritual death, as a result of a choice He made possible. We have also looked at many places in scripture when He continues allowing people to make self-destructive choices in their lives, choices that God did not approve.

We saw that the people of Israel rejected God's Kingship as well as His liberty and chose a human government, a king, despite God's warning of what conditions would come on them from kings.

We saw that God restrained His power many times throughout history, including when Jesus tells Pilate that He could call on a army of angels to spare him from Pilate's hand but He did not.

Liberty is love. God loves us and so He allows us to make our own choices, even to reject Him, even to our own destruction.

We have also known about the terrible crimes that governments have perpetrated against people across the centuries and across the world.

This becomes very confusing when we then look at Romans 13. If you have not read the first half of this book some of this may not make sense.

On first reading of the text in English it appears to instruct Christians in an absolute submission to governing authorities and it appears to claim that all those in authority are good and just. And finally, that they are all put into their positions by God's choice. This would seem to put any resistance by Christians in the same camp as Korah in the wilderness rebelling against Moses, God's anointed. Is that really what Paul is trying to say here?

If this is indeed the meaning of this passage then no Christian should have supported the Declaration of Independence and the Revolutionary war. Further, Christians in Germany would never - been approved by God to resist or oppose the Third Reich.

Is the text truly meaning to tell us that all rulers or authorities are anointed by God? Or is there a measure, such as fruit, when the

Christian may judge that a ruler or authority does not carry that anointing?

Does the text mean all authorities down to the most trivial, even homeowner's associations and husbands? Are we not also under the rule of the great commandments to love God and love our neighbor as ourselves?

Is there room in this passage for exceptions? What if the ruler or authority abuses those that he is charged in assisting or supporting? Can the people just an authority by this fruit and decline to submit if his fruit is harmful?

God hates divorce. Scripture teaches a wife to submit to her husband. What if a wife and / or children resist him and run away due to abuse? Scripture does not address this reasoning.

> And when they had summoned them, they commanded them not to speak or teach at all in the name of Jesus. But Peter and John answered and said to them, "Whether it is right in the sight of God to give heed to you rather than to God, you be the judge; for we cannot stop speaking about what we have seen and heard." When they had threatened them further, they let them go (finding no basis on which to punish them) on account of the people, because they were all glorifying God for what had happened; for the man was more than forty years old on whom this miracle of healing had been performed. - Acts 4:18-22

The fact that Christians were persecuted is evidence that they were acting in opposition to the local authorities from the first century.

So there are instances when Christians may judge that governing authorities are acting in opposition to God.

REVIVAL, HOLINESS, & LIBERTY

Throughout the history of the Church, few movements have carried the intensity, sincerity, and transformative power of revival. From the wilderness revivals of early America to the great awakenings that shook nations, the cry of revival has always centered on one thing: a return to God. Revival is not merely a renewal of religious enthusiasm—it is the breaking of the human heart under the weight of God's presence and the freeing of the soul from its bondage to sin. But revival, in its most powerful form, always awakens a question of liberty. What do we do with our newfound spiritual freedom? Do we preserve liberty, or do we try to enforce holiness?

Every revival in history has been marked by common traits: deep repentance, public confession of sin, intense hunger for God's Word, and a desire to live a pure and righteous life. These revivals often began not in great cathedrals, but in humble homes, open-air meetings, and prayer gatherings. Revival is deeply personal before it ever becomes public. It starts in the heart of an individual who is desperate for God and unwilling to settle for casual religion.

In Scripture, we see revivals occur when the people of God realize how far they have drifted and cry out for renewal. In the time of Nehemiah and Ezra, a revival took place when the Word of God was read aloud and the people responded with weeping, fasting, and obedience. The result was national transformation—not through coercion, but through conviction.

In the same way, the revivals in American history—particularly the First and Second Great Awakenings—were grassroots movements of spiritual renewal. They emphasized personal conversion, moral transformation, and a passionate walk with God. But something else often occurred in the wake of these revivals: a growing desire among believers to shape society in the image of the holiness they had found.

THE SECOND GREAT AWAKENING AND PERSONAL HOLINESS

The Second Great Awakening, which spanned from the 1790s to the 1840s, was perhaps the most socially influential revival in American history. It democratized American Christianity, gave rise to new denominations, and birthed widespread evangelical fervor. It was marked by camp meetings, emotional preaching, and a call to individual repentance.

Preachers such as Charles Finney emphasized the moral responsibility of individuals to respond to God's call. Finney's messages were uncompromising in their call to holiness and faith, yet they often carried a reforming edge. He, like many revivalists, believed that true conversion would lead to social action. The result was the rise of abolitionist movements, women's suffrage advocates, and anti-alcohol campaigns. These were not fringe responses. They were expressions of a sincere belief that a holy people would build a holy society.

Yet, herein lies the tension. While God absolutely calls His people to live holy lives, He does not call them to enforce holiness upon others by coercion. Holiness must always remain the fruit of the Spirit, not the result of civil legislation or cultural pressure. Liberty is preserved only when individuals are free to respond to God's Spirit—not when laws are crafted to make sinners behave like saints.

HOLINESS AND THE RISE OF AUTHORITARIAN REFORM

The Holiness movement of the 19th century sprang forth from the soil of the Second Great Awakening. Rooted in the Methodist tradition and the teachings of John Wesley, the movement sought what it called "entire sanctification", a second work of grace beyond conversion that purged the believer of sin and filled them with divine love.

Leaders such as Phoebe Palmer and later denominations like the Church of the Nazarene and the Free Methodist Church carried this vision forward. The hallmark of the movement was its insistence that holiness was not only possible—it was necessary. The power of God was available to transform the heart fully, not just partially.

The fruit of this belief was beautiful in many ways. Lives were changed. Addictions were broken. Families were restored. Many of these believers extended their transformed lives into acts of service, missions, and justice. They saw no conflict between personal holiness and social activism. They believed that to love God was also to love neighbor, and that meant confronting societal sins like slavery, inequality, and addiction.

But there was also a dangerous edge to this fervor. As the movement gained influence, its leaders and adherents sometimes crossed the line between persuasion and pressure. The belief that society should reflect Christian morality led to partnerships with political movements that sought to legislate behavior. Nowhere was this more evident than in the Prohibition movement.

PROHIBITION: WHEN HOLINESS BECAME LAW

By the early 20th century, the Holiness movement's alignment with the temperance cause had become a defining mark of its social engagement. Alcohol, viewed as a destroyer of families and a corrupter of moral character, became the chief target of their reform efforts.

To be sure, the effects of alcohol abuse were devastating in many communities. Taverns were often centers of violence, poverty, and vice. Holiness preachers saw abstinence from alcohol as essential to a life fully surrendered to God.

> But rather than continue addressing the issue through moral teaching and discipleship, they joined forces with political groups to push for national legislation.

The result was the 18th Amendment and the Volstead Act—ushering in Prohibition in 1920.

This was a bold attempt to enforce holiness through law. The Holiness movement, in many ways, had succeeded politically, but spiritually, the victory was incomplete. The amendment did little to change hearts. Instead, it gave rise to illegal markets, organized crime, and a deep national ambivalence toward government-imposed morality. Eventually, Prohibition was repealed in 1933, and the lesson was clear. You can outlaw behavior, but you cannot legislate righteousness.

THE DIFFERENCE BETWEEN INNER HOLINESS AND OUTER CONTROL

God is deeply committed to holiness. He calls His people to be holy as He is holy (1 Peter 1:16). He gives His Spirit to guide, convict, and empower believers to live lives of purity, love, and obedience. Holiness is not optional—it is the expected fruit of true discipleship.

But the mistake comes when holiness is turned outward as a tool for social control. In God's economy, holiness is always a response to grace, not a requirement for acceptance. And liberty—true liberty—means that every person must have the freedom to respond to God voluntarily and even say 'No'.

> *This is the heart of God's character. He gave humanity free will even though He knew we might misuse it. He offered the law to Israel not as a tool of coercion but as a guide for living in covenant relationship with Him. And in Christ, He gave the ultimate example of love—not forcing obedience but inviting surrender.*

When human systems attempt to enforce godliness from the outside—through law, punishment, or political pressure, they step into authoritarianism. It is one thing for a person to say, "As for me and my house, we will serve the Lord," and quite another to say, "As for this nation, you will serve the Lord—or else." The first is biblical leadership; the second is spiritual tyranny.

REVIVAL AND THE PRESERVATION OF LIBERTY

The irony is that revival, when truly sent by God, always increases liberty. The heart that has encountered God is no longer bound by sin or societal pressure. It is free. Free to worship. Free to obey. Free to love. This is the liberty of the sons and daughters of God, not a liberty to do whatever pleases them, but a liberty to do what pleases Him.

The Apostle Paul captures this beautifully in Galatians 5:1:

"It is for freedom that Christ has set us free. Stand firm, then, and do not let yourselves be burdened again by a yoke of slavery.

The Galatians were being tempted to return to legalism, thinking that righteousness could be secured through rule-keeping. Paul rebukes this, affirming that holiness must come from the Spirit, not from the law.

Likewise, revival must never become a cover for reintroducing religious law into public policy. **Holiness must be modeled, not mandated**. The Church's greatest witness is not its power in politics, but its purity in practice.

LESSONS FROM HISTORY—AND WARNINGS FOR TODAY

As we reflect on the legacy of revival and the Holiness movement, we are left with both inspiration and caution. The courage of men and women who pursued holiness with sincerity and passion is a testimony worth emulating. Their acts of compassion, sacrifice, and justice reshaped nations. But the temptation to seize the levers of political power in order to impose that holiness on others is a mistake we must not repeat.

In today's polarized climate, some again seek to align revival with nationalism or to enforce Christian ethics through legal means. Yet history and Scripture both teach that the Kingdom of God does not advance through coercion, but through conversion. Revival is not a legislative agenda—it is a spiritual awakening.

To preserve both revival and liberty, we must keep holiness in its rightful place. It is the goal of the Christian life, the fruit of God's Spirit, and the expression of a heart surrendered to Jesus. But it must never become a weapon to dominate others. Our calling is to proclaim the gospel, live holy lives, and trust that the same Spirit who transformed us is able to transform others as well—if they are free to choose.

HOW EDUCATION UNDERMINED LIBERTY

If you send your children to Caesar for education do not be surprised when they return as Romans.

So many people are wondering what has become of the American education system in this century. What if I told you that it was designed this way 180 years ago? It was not a conspiracy. It was not even a secret. It was the work of true believers done in the light of day and the public eye with all good intentions. It was done by elitists who believed that they knew what was best for children to learn in this relatively young republic. Would you stay with me to the end of this to see what I mean?

Ask anyone around you if you were required to read either or both of the Federalist Papers or the Anti-Federalist papers in any of your history classes in school. Most people have heard of the Federalist Papers. Some had been required to read them in high school. Few remembered anything about them. Fewer still had even heard of the Anti-Federalist papers. The Federalist Papers written in support of a strong central government to which the states should delegate some of their sovereignty. Anti-Federalists opposed such an idea largely under the suspicion of what such a large central government could grow into over time.

The lack of awareness of 20th-21st century Americans of their own history and foundational beliefs about liberty reveals one of many biases that have been present in the American school system for over 180 years. It was never about liberty for the organizers of American schools. It was about compliance to government and business. It was about removing any tendencies toward critical or independent thinking. Let me explain.

The common rhetoric about America's founding as told in American schools, paints a romantic picture of a unified group of men working to craft a constitution that would protect the people's lives, liberties, and pursuit of happiness. The truth is that they were very far from unified. There was great disagreement within many early Presidential administrations over how much Constitutional power the central government has.

By the middle of the 19th century, there were some who claimed that the residents of the thirteen states were largely ignorant and illiterate. They used this argument to justify a US government sponsored school system. Their argument was false. In fact, nearly all white European men were well educated in reading, mathematics, history, philosophy, music, art, and agriculture. This enabled Hamilton and Madison to publish the Federalist Papers attempting to persuade the populace to support the new Constitution and central government as well as the authors of the Anti-Federalist papers to counter them with their own persuasion.

Private and religious education was common in the colonies from long before the revolution. Nearly all the colonists who had come over from England were already practiced in reading the Bible. Many also were well read in the ancient Greek classics like Homer, Cicero, Plato, and others. Such teaching continued privately and through churches throughout the colonies. Some communities raised funds voluntarily for their own local schools. There was very little distinction in the average American's mind at that time between religious schools, private schools, and community schools. Nearly all used the Bible and Greek literature for their curriculum.

In the thirty years between 1820 and 1850 a couple of million immigrants from Europe flowed into America, nearly half from Ireland and a substantial number were Catholic. Until that time America had been dominated by protestants. This led to some of the similar rivalries and hostilities that had plagued both groups in Europe since the Protestant reformation in the 16th century. Besides Catholic churches rising where none had been, Catholic schools were also expanding in cities and settlements. Over this period there arose a new view about religious schools distinct from community schools. A belief grew that Catholics were more loyal to the Pope than to America.

Some began to see a need for an American identity school. That is, schools that would teach foundational principles of what made America unique. Given the Protestant influence dominant in the US, the new American schools, "Public Schools", started out using Protestant hymns, prayers, and the King James Bible. Later, these items faded out in favor of a non-religious civic virtue curriculum.

The narrative of the Public Schools was the Federalist view of the benefits of a central government over all the states. This was accelerated after the war between the states when the 10th amendment became impotent and largely forgotten. There was little discussion about liberty.

While not the earliest assault on liberty, there came one from Massachusetts that remains with us today, government schools. Certainly, anyone who has spent time in Massachusetts is well aware of their long history of authoritarianism.

As with many authoritarians, their ideas can sound excellent. They can be articulate and persuasive. In the first half of the 19th century, many were becoming increasingly concerned about education and schools. Education and schooling are not the same thing. A child may grow up in an agricultural home and become educated in the things necessary for a farm to succeed and prosper. That child is becoming educated in important things but may not know how to read. Education is the learning from the sum total of human knowledge. Schooling on the other hand is the control of what is learned, how it is learned and who teaches it.

Horace Mann (1796-1859), considered by many to be the father of the American school system, was the first Secretary of Education overseeing the first State board of Education in the country. This happened in Massachusetts in 1835. The purpose for Mann and this board was to develop a universal education process for the children of Massachusetts.

In addition to traditional subjects such as reading, writing, and arithmetic, there was strong sentiment pushing for teaching the fundamentals of a democratic republic. He started out in agreement with Thomas Jefferson believing that no republic can endure unless its citizens are literate and educated. Underlying that, education was a strong belief in morals and civic virtue.

As noted above, the nation was experiencing a new diversity in the first half of the 19th century. This introduced a variation in values and understanding what the new nation was about. Further, the founding generation was aging out leaving the next generation in place who had not experienced the oppression by the British crown that had led to the revolution. Religious, ethnic, language and political differences were coming to the shores of the new nation.

Mann had heard for many years about the success of the Prussian educational model. In 1843, he traveled there to find out what this was about and to learn their techniques.

Prussia was one of the European states that later merged to become Germany. In 1806 they fought a bloody war defending themselves unsuccessfully from the armies of Napoleon. The Prussian army had had great success in wars in the prior century under Frederick, the Great, but had become fragmented since then with multiple chains of command. Many younger soldiers had little training and were deciding for themselves how and when to fight and when to obey orders or not.

After that war with Napoleon, they undertook a process of reforming their military by reforming their educational system beginning with young children. This process was strongly influenced by Johann Fichte, a German philosopher. The Monarchy of Prussia sought to instill strict social obedience in their citizens. Every citizen must be thoroughly convinced that the King was always just and right, and that social obedience was of highest importance. They designed their school system to instill loyalty to the government and to train young men for the military or for government bureaucracy. Fichte said, "The schools must fashion the person, and fashion him in such a way that he simply cannot will otherwise than what you wish him to will."

Mandatory government school attendance by all children between five and thirteen had already been implemented in Prussia by 1763. Such compulsory schooling combined with the reforms after the war unified the country under common principles of duty, discipline, respect for authority, and to follow orders.

"Education should aim at destroying free will so that after pupils are thus schooled, they will be incapable throughout the rest of their lives of thinking or acting otherwise than as their school masters would have wished." – Johann Fichte

"The Prussian mind, which carried the day, held a clear idea of what centralized schooling should deliver:

1) Obedient soldiers to the army.

2) Obedient workers for mines, factories, and farms.

3) Well-subordinated civil servants trained in their function.

4) Well-subordinated clerks for industry.

5) Citizens who thought alike on most issues.

6) National uniformity in thought, word, and deed." [1]

- John Taylor Gatto

Horace Mann returned from Prussia and set about lobbying the state government of Massachusetts to implement these methods and practices. By 1852, Massachusetts was the first state to implement free and mandatory school attendance for elementary school. Other reforms Mann implemented during this time included teacher training. New teachers in colleges in Massachusetts were trained in common curriculum in every subject. The state chose and composed the curriculum that every child would learn which supported the principles of the Prussian model.

A year after Massachusetts adopted the Prussian model, New York followed. The governor of New York at the time had received his PhD from a university in Prussia as did many other political and social leaders in the 19th century.

As noted previously, Mann was a supporter of many of Thomas Jefferson's ideas about the role of government and education. Mann had great intentions to instill in students in government schools the values of democracy and the Constitution. He wanted the students to grow up with a love for country and government that leads it.

His goals could easily be seen as positive and beneficial both for students and for the nation.

However, his methods were very much that of an authoritarian. The words mandatory, obedience, unquestioning, conformity, uniformity and many synonyms must send chills down the spine of everyone who understands and loves liberty. Mann brought an authoritarian practice of schooling run by government to the US. He advocated for a state (government) based school system where the state decides what the child should learn, how and when they should learn it. He created an army of teachers trained in such conformity, uniformity, and compliance. These teachers became administrators and politicians and leaders spreading their authoritarian model across the country. By 1900 every state had the same mandatory schooling model. By 1900 nearly all PhDs in America were earned at universities in Prussia/Germany.

Are we surprised that America's school system is so very authoritarian and breeds so many authoritarians?

The curriculum they developed and used in these mandatory schools carried a single view portraying the state and federal governments as good and moral and right. They reinforced the Federalist model of a powerful central government as protector and even savior of the people.

How is it that Americans have allowed so many violations of their natural and Constitutional rights from the very beginning of the republic? How is it that so many Americans have conformed and obeyed governments at local, state, and federal levels in the recent virus outbreak. Government, health officials, and the media seek to use legal and social force to gain compliance to a common agenda. Our American school system has created this conformity and obedience.

THE AMERICAN SCHOOL SYSTEM IS THE HEART AND SOUL OF AUTHORITARIANISM.

It crushes critical thinking. It either paints romantic notions about government and law enforcement or uses authoritarianism to paint the govt and law enforcement as all totalitarian and supremacist. Teaching degrees and credentials ensure that the uniformity, conformity, and obedience values are transmitted to the students. A common curriculum of history limits access by students to the "rest of the story". The mandatory nature of schools reinforces authoritarianism as the preferred model for achievement and success.

Liberty is either hidden or redefined. Students are taught that they live in the "land of the free" from within a mandatory, authoritarian structure. Students are taught that our military is fighting for our liberty overseas. Yet our schools are educating our students against liberty at home.

To restore any concept of liberty in schooling in the US we must separate school and state. That means abolishing the Federal Department of Education and each state's similar department and return control of schools to local and parental control and even equip more families for private and homeschooling.

EDUCATION AS DISCIPLESHIP IN THE KINGDOM OF GOD

In the Kingdom of God, education is not a separate sphere from discipleship. Jesus Himself was called Rabbi—Teacher. His Great Commission commands us to "make disciples of all nations... teaching them to observe all I have commanded you" (Matthew 28:19-20). Kingdom-minded education must therefore include the formation of character, the development of discernment, and the cultivation of a mind renewed by truth.

This is the kind of education that produces free people: people who are free from the bondage of lies, sin, and fear; people who are free to love, serve, and build; people who know whose they are and why they exist.

A Biblically grounded education teaches:

- That truth is not invented but discovered, because it flows from God

- That liberty is God's plan for His people.

- That knowledge must serve love, and love must be rooted in liberty and truth

This kind of education cannot be mass-produced. It must be intentional, relational, and anchored in God's Word. It must resist the pressures of conformity and affirm the dignity and uniqueness of every child.

THE DANGER OF AUTHORITARIAN EDUCATION

When education becomes centralized, rigid, and ideologically narrow, it ceases to be education and becomes indoctrination. The authoritarian models of education found in totalitarian regimes— whether fascist or Marxist—always begin with control over schools. Why? Because if you shape the minds of children, you shape the future of a nation.

We must ask: Is modern American education trending toward liberty or toward control? Are we raising critical thinkers or compliant consumers? Are we fostering courage or conformity?

The Kingdom-minded Christian cannot be neutral here. If we believe that liberty is sacred because it reflects God's gift of moral agency, then we must oppose any system, educational or otherwise, that undermines that gift.

THE ROLE OF THE CHURCH IN EDUCATION

The early Church understood education as a core aspect of its mission. Catechism, apprenticeship, and the reading of Scripture were central. Today, the Church must reclaim this role. Pastors and congregations must encourage and equip families to take education seriously as a spiritual endeavor.

Churches can support:

- Homeschooling families with resources, prayer, and encouragement

- Christian schools with funding and volunteerism

- Public school families with discernment tools and after-school discipleship

Whatever the context, the Church must not be silent about education. Silence cedes ground to secularism. Engagement reclaims ground for the Kingdom.

PASSING LIBERTY ON: THE INTERGENERATIONAL MISSION

Ronald Reagan famously said that liberty is never more than one generation away from extinction. The same is true for Kingdom values. If we do not teach our children what is true, beautiful, and good, the world will teach them what is false, ugly, and destructive.

Education is therefore not just about the present. It is about the future. Every child formed in truth is a carrier of liberty. Every student who knows Christ is a potential reformer, peacemaker, and builder of God's Kingdom.

This is the mission: to pass on not just knowledge, but wisdom; not just freedom, but virtue; not just literacy, but love.

If liberty is to endure in America, it must be taught by parents and teachers and books. But more than taught, it must be caught, modeled by parents, lived out by teachers, and reinforced by communities of faith.

Education is not neutral. It is spiritual. It is a battleground of allegiance and imagination. The question is not whether children will be shaped, but *how* and *by whom*. Kingdom-minded Christians must rise to this moment with courage, clarity, and compassion.

Let us therefore teach the truth. Let us model liberty. Let us reclaim education not as a tool of the state, but as an instrument of the Kingdom of God. For where the Spirit of the Lord is, there is liberty. And it is that liberty, grounded in truth and lived in love, that will truly make our children free.

———

[1] *The Underground History of American Education* John Taylor Gatto, NY State Teacher of the Year 1991

LIBERTY ACROSS GENERATIONS

"Freedom is never more than one generation away from extinction. We didn't pass it to our children in the bloodstream. It must be fought for, protected, and handed on for them to do the same, or one day we will spend our sunset years telling our children and our children's children what it was once like in the United States where men were free." - Ronald Reagan

Train up a child in the way he should go,
Even when he is old, he will not depart from it.
-Proverbs 22:6

Freedom is not a genetic inheritance. It is not a permanent fixture in human civilization, nor a given just because it once was. It is an idea—fragile, potent, and always at risk. The quote from Reagan is not a poetic exaggeration. It is a sober warning to every generation that the liberty they enjoy must be intentionally passed on or it will vanish.

But how can we pass on liberty if we don't teach it? How can children grow up to love freedom if all they witness is authoritarianism and provision? If a child grows up under constant control, surrounded by safety nets and dependent on authority figures for every need, how will they ever learn to stand on their own two feet? More importantly, how will they learn to value liberty enough to protect it?

LESSONS FROM UTOPIAN SOCIALISM

In the 1830s, a wave of experimental communities rose up in the United States, particularly in regions like Ohio, Kentucky, and Tennessee. These utopian groups believed in the radical ideal of equality in all things, property, labor, and rewards. They were founded on the principle of voluntary communal sharing: shared tools, shared labor, and shared benefits.

By today's definitions, we would classify these groups as socialist. Yet, while they burned bright for a short time, most did not survive beyond a single generation. Why? The first generation of settlers chose the experiment willingly. They agreed on a set of ideals and entered the community with the expectation of mutual contribution and benefit. Their sacrifice was voluntary, and their unity was driven by shared conviction.

But their children and grandchildren were born into this system without choice. They didn't voluntarily sign on to the social contract. And as they matured, many of them began to see the cracks. They noticed that while everyone was expected to share equally in the fruit of labor, not everyone labored equally. Some worked tirelessly, while others coasted. Yet all received the same. The system punished industriousness and rewarded idleness. Over time, disillusionment grew. The children began to ask, "Why should I work harder than the next person if there's no difference in the outcome?"

This tension between imposed equality and earned reward fractured these communities. Without a personal conviction for the shared ideals, the next generation rejected the sacrifices of their parents. Voluntary generosity degenerated into perceived coercion. Liberty, when replaced with enforced equity, begins to rot from within.

This story is not just a footnote in American history. It's a parable for the danger every free society faces. When liberty is not taught and internalized, it is easily replaced by comfort, security, and ultimately control.

AUTHORITARIANISM AND PROVISION: A SUBTLE PAIRING

Humans are not naturally inclined toward liberty. Left to our own devices, we tend to choose safety over risk, provision over independence, certainty over self-determination. This is a survival instinct. From our earliest days, we are nurtured, protected, and cared for by those stronger than us. We grow up seeing authority figures—parents, teachers, coaches, administrators—not just as sources of discipline, but also as sources of provision.

This pairing of control and care teaches us a powerful lesson: authority brings safety. And so, unless we are taught otherwise, we come to believe that the path to security is through submission to authority. We trade our freedom for comfort, our responsibility for provision.

This lesson begins in childhood. Children require adult guidance— no one questions this. Boundaries, rules, discipline, and provision are necessary for healthy development. A young child cannot survive without the oversight of an adult. Parents must use their authority to teach, correct, and protect.

But somewhere along the way, the goal must shift. As children grow, the aim of parenting must change from control to empowerment and independence. If children are never given the opportunity to fail, to struggle, to bear the weight of consequences, they will never learn to choose wisely. They will forever look for someone else to make their choices and bear their burdens. This is not love. It is bondage masked as protection.

THE MISSING LESSONS: INDEPENDENCE AND RESPONSIBILITY

Too often, parents misunderstand the meaning of love. In an effort to protect their children from the pain they themselves experienced, they shield them from adversity. They clean up every mess, smooth every rough edge, and fight every battle on their child's behalf.

This style of parenting may come from a good heart, but it produces weak character. It teaches children that someone else will always clean up the mess. It delays maturity. And it cultivates dependency.

Adversity is not the enemy. In fact, adversity is one of life's greatest teachers. Personal experience, especially painful experience, is vivid and memorable. It teaches lessons that lectures never can. A scraped knee teaches caution. A failed test teaches preparation. A broken friendship teaches empathy and honesty. These are the raw materials from which personal responsibility is forged.

If children are never allowed to face difficulty, they are denied the opportunity to grow. Independence is not granted, it is earned. And it is earned through trial, error, and perseverance.

The tension between authority and liberty in the home has become increasingly apparent in recent decades. Terms like "helicopter parenting" and "free-range parenting" reflect two opposing philosophies.

Helicopter parents are those who hover. They manage every detail of their child's life, protect them from every possible danger, and intervene at the slightest hint of discomfort. While this might feel like love, it communicates a different message: "You are not capable."

This overbearing protection stifles independence. It delays the development of decision-making skills. It teaches children to outsource responsibility and reinforces the idea that safety must be provided by others.

In contrast, free-range parents understand that risk is a part of life. They gradually increase the freedoms granted to their children, allowing them to explore, to try, and sometimes to fail. This approach does not ignore danger—it respects it. But it also respects the child's ability to grow and adapt.

As Jordan Peterson wisely asked, "Do you want to make your children safe, or strong?" You cannot do both. Strength is forged in the fire of experience. A safe environment can produce comfort—but rarely courage. If our children never face resistance, they will never develop the resilience needed to defend liberty.

THE ALLURE OF THE NANNY STATE

Here lies the great danger: children raised without liberty will not seek it. They will not long for what they never tasted. Instead, when they leave the care of their parents, they will look for new providers, new authorities to shield them from risk and responsibility. And most often, that provider is the state.

The government becomes a new parent. It offers comfort, provision, and safety in exchange for obedience. Citizens raised without personal responsibility will naturally gravitate toward authoritarian systems, especially those that promise equity and security. But this is not freedom. It is dependency dressed in noble language.

When weakness is cultivated, slavery is inevitable. When strength is cultivated, liberty becomes possible.

The goal, then, must be to raise children who are strong, independent, and capable. Who know how to think for themselves, to work, to strive, to sacrifice, and to take responsibility for their own lives. These are the citizens who will cherish and protect liberty.

TEACHING THE VALUE OF LIBERTY

The challenge of liberty is that it must be chosen. It cannot be imposed. And it cannot be passed down by inheritance. Each generation must embrace it for themselves. Which means each generation must be taught—not just the *idea* of liberty, but its *cost* and its *responsibilities*.

We must teach our children that liberty is not license. It is not the freedom to do whatever one wants. True liberty requires virtue. It requires self-governance. It demands that individuals restrain their own impulses for the good of others and for the preservation of liberty itself. True liberty respects other people's sovereignty over their bodies, labor, earnings and property. True liberty knows its limits. One person's liberty extends to the limits of the liberty of their neighbor. Loving your neighbor means respecting their liberty. Liberty is love.

Liberty without virtue becomes anarchy. And anarchy always collapses into tyranny.

That's why teaching liberty involves teaching history. Children must understand the sacrifices made by those who came before them. They must learn about the tyrannies that were overthrown and the freedoms that were won. They must understand that freedom was bought with blood and that it can be lost through neglect.

We must tell them the stories of those who stood against oppression, of Washington, Jefferson, Douglass, King. We must show them what courage looks like. We must help them see that the freedom they enjoy is not normal in human history. It is rare, and it is precious.

Liberty is not taught through slogans. It is modeled in daily life. Children learn not just through words, but through the examples set by those closest to them.

If parents value liberty, they must model it. They must demonstrate personal responsibility. They must allow natural consequences to take their course. They must provide opportunities for decision-making and autonomy—even when it involves risk.

They must also model respect for others' freedom. Children should see parents honoring the choices and boundaries of others, even when they disagree. They should see charity and grace toward those who fail. They should see sacrifice, perseverance, and courage.

A home that cultivates liberty will not always be tidy. It will involve failure, frustration, and struggle. But it will also produce strength, resilience, and wisdom. These are the fruits of liberty.

THE GENERATIONAL CHALLENGE

We are always one generation away from losing freedom. That is not just rhetorical. It is historical truth. Every society that forgot to teach liberty lost it. Every people that traded freedom for comfort fell into tyranny.

The question we must ask is: what kind of adults are we raising? Will they be strong or weak? Independent or dependent? Free or enslaved?

If we want to preserve liberty, we must teach it. We must model it. We must value it more than comfort. And we must let our children taste the dignity of standing on their own, of making choices, of facing consequences, of rising after failure, and of building a life with their own hands.

Freedom is not the absence of hardship. It is the presence of dignity, responsibility, and hope. It is a gift. But it is a gift that must be chosen—by every generation, for themselves.

Let us be the generation that teaches liberty again.

HOW SHOULD WE THEN LIVE?

KINGDOM MINDED

"Jesus talked more about the Kingdom of God than any other single topic."

This striking truth should cause every follower of Jesus to pause. For those who claim His name, to be ignorant of His most emphasized teaching is to risk misrepresenting Him altogether. If we desire to follow Jesus faithfully, not just in worship, but in lifestyle and worldview we must grasp what it means to live as a Kingdom-minded Christian.

Too often, Christian teaching has focused on escaping this world, waiting passively for heaven or Christ's return, treating earthly existence as a temporary nuisance. But that is not how Jesus spoke of our mission. When He taught His disciples to pray, He didn't say, "Take us quickly to heaven," but rather:

"Your kingdom come. Your will be done, On earth as it is in heaven."
Matthew 6:10

This is a dangerous prayer for anyone unwilling to participate in its fulfillment. It is not a passive desire. It is a petition for transformation, both inward and societal. Jesus did not teach escapism. He taught engagement. The Kingdom of God is not merely a future promise; it is a present calling. The reign of Christ begins in the hearts of those who submit to Him and spreads like leaven, invisibly permeating society from within.

Jesus' ministry began with a declaration: *"Repent, for the Kingdom of Heaven is at hand!"* (Matthew 4:17). He did not speak of an abstract theological category or a distant utopia, but of something active and near, something so immediate that it demanded a response. Every parable, healing, confrontation, and teaching was about unveiling what that Kingdom looks like in practice.

And yet, Jesus also said, *"My kingdom is not of this world"* (John 18:36). It is not enforced by swords, by politics, or by domination. It is a Kingdom unlike any on earth: it rules through hearts, not laws; through consent, not coercion; through self-sacrificing love, not state-imposed morality.

To live as Kingdom-minded Christians, we must embrace this radically different model of influence.

LIBERTY AS A KINGDOM VALUE

Throughout this book, we have emphasized a crucial truth: liberty is not a modern political invention. It is a Kingdom principle rooted in the very nature of God.

From the Garden of Eden, God granted Adam and Eve the liberty to choose, even the freedom to choose wrongly. God, who could control all things, instead allowed for rebellion. He did not install electric fences around the forbidden tree. He did not make obedience the only available option. Why?

Because forced obedience is not love. Coerced faith is not faith at all.

Liberty is essential for love to be genuine and for obedience to be meaningful.

A Kingdom-minded Christian must recognize that the sovereignty of the individual, though often misused, is God-given. Without sovereignty, there can be no real surrender. And without surrender, there is no true relationship with God.

> *"I call heaven and earth to witness against you today, that I have set before you life and death, the blessing and the curse. So choose life..." (Deuteronomy 30:19)*

Choice lies at the core of divine-human interaction.

DO NOT REMOVE TEMPTATIONS BY FORCE

Many Christians, in the name of righteousness, seek to remove temptations from society through the force of law or government intervention. While well-intentioned, this often leads to the erosion of liberty and to the rise of authoritarianism masquerading as morality.

God, in His holiness, allows temptation to exist.

Jesus Himself was "led up by the Spirit into the wilderness to be tempted by the devil" (Matthew 4:1). If God does not shelter His own Son from temptation, how dare we think we are wiser than God by forcibly removing temptation from others?

When Christians legislate against every form of sin—not merely to protect victims, but to suppress the capacity for individuals to choose—we cease to represent the Kingdom and begin to act like tyrants. We begin to rule like Pharaoh, not like Christ.

THE ROLE OF CONSENT

Kingdom values affirm consent. God never overrides a person's free will, and neither should we. This is a foundational ethic:

Do not initiate force except in defense of the innocent.

Do not override someone else's consent regarding their own body, labor, earnings, or property.

Do not claim authority over what is not yours.

Even when our motivations are noble, our methods must remain godly. The ends do not justify the means in the Kingdom of God. Coercion is not a tool of righteousness.

WHAT BELONGS TO YOU?

Jesus said, *"Render to Caesar the things that are Caesar's, and to God the things that are God's"* (Mark 12:17). This wasn't a statement about taxes alone. It was a challenge about rightful ownership. What truly belongs to Caesar? What truly belongs to God?

Too often, we blur these lines. In the name of civic duty or religious influence, we claim dominion over what is not ours. A Kingdom-minded Christian must vigilantly discern what is theirs to control and what is not:

You are sovereign over your own body.

You are responsible for your labor and how it is used.

You are accountable for your earnings and your property.

You are not sovereign over your neighbor's body, choices, or worship.

Understanding this division of stewardship creates humility. It restrains the impulse to dominate others "for their own good." It produces a community of mutual respect rather than mutual regulation.

Liberty and Trust

Liberty thrives in an atmosphere of trust.

In a society shaped by the Kingdom of God, people respect boundaries. They honor one another's privacy. They do not steal, covet, or manipulate. When a person of liberty finds someone's private journal on a table, they do not read it. Not because they fear punishment—but because they honor the dignity of the other person.

This is the fruit of internal transformation, not external regulation.

Jesus said, *"Out of the abundance of the heart the mouth speaks"* (Matthew 12:34). The Kingdom does not change people from the outside in. It works from the inside out.

KINGDOM VALUES AND CIVIL AUTHORITY

The early church understood how to live under unjust governments without compromising Kingdom values. Peter and John, when forbidden to preach Jesus, responded:

> *"Whether it is right in the sight of God to listen to you rather than to God, you must judge." (Acts 4:19)*

They did not riot. They did not overthrow the Sanhedrin. But neither did they comply. They obeyed God rather than men.

Likewise, Daniel and his companions did not wage war against Babylon. But when ordered to eat forbidden food, to bow to idols, or to cease prayer, they respectfully refused—even at the cost of their lives.

Kingdom-minded Christians are not anarchists. But they are not blind patriots either. They discern when earthly authority demands allegiance that belongs to God, and they resist—not with hatred, but with holiness.

Modern democracies offer Christians a rare opportunity: participation. When you vote, you are exercising delegated authority over others. A Kingdom-minded Christian must ask: *Am I voting in a way that reflects God's Kingdom or man's coercion?*

Are my votes protecting liberty or expanding control?

Am I supporting policies that punish sin or that promote human dignity?

Do I favor candidates who trust the people or who seek to rule them?

Even when Christians disagree on specific policies, this foundational lens, liberty rooted in Kingdom ethics, should guide every political action.

TAXES, ZONING, AND LIBERTY

In our current systems, Christians must navigate complex issues such as taxation, zoning, and public policy. A Kingdom-minded framework invites critical reflection:

Taxes, when excessive or coercive, can become a violation of one's labor and earnings. The Bible does not explicitly condemn all taxes, but it does condemn exploitation and injustice. Injustice can be found when a homeowner can lose their home when the state confiscates it for non-payment of taxes even when the house is fully paid for.

Taxation is an override of consent. The majority decides and any dissenters must still comply. Taxation is necessary in a society where the majority do not want to allow anyone to opt out.

HOW DO WE DEAL WITH OVERRIDING CONSENT IN A DEMOCRATIC SOCIETY?

Now, in modern democracies like the U.S., taxation is enforced regardless of your individual consent, even if you vote against it.

This seems to contradict the principle of consent. So how do we resolve it? Here's one way to frame it.

In God's Kingdom, no person's property or labor is seized without consent. In man's kingdoms, consent is diluted through representative systems and majority rule.

Thus:

- **Christian ethics should hold that ideal before us—** consensual governance, voluntary contribution, shared stewardship.

- **Civic participation is the tool we are given** in democracy to push society closer to those ideals.

But even in democracy, **being outvoted does not equal personal moral consent** and the Christian may still regard involuntary taxation as coercion, even while submitting to it peacefully.

Zoning laws, though often presented as promoting order, can in some cases amount to government theft, regulating private property in ways that benefit bureaucrats more than communities. Often neighbors seek to control through law what their neighbors do with their private property. This is not from God. God does not override consent.

The Kingdom value is this: **property is sacred**. The labor of the individual is to be honored. If we seek justice, it must be done without violating the sovereignty of others.

LEAVEN, NOT FORCE

Jesus used a beautiful metaphor for how the Kingdom spreads:

"The kingdom of heaven is like leaven, which a woman took and hid in three pecks of flour until it was all leavened." (Matthew 13:33)

Leaven does not explode into bread with fanfare. It works quietly. Invisibly. It transforms from within.

The Kingdom grows the same way. It changes individuals, who then change families, workplaces, and cities. It does not march with armies or campaign with slogans. It moves through love, integrity, humility, and mercy. It spreads by sacrifice, not domination.

This is the model for how we bring the Kingdom into every area of life—from education to economics, from art to agriculture.

FINAL ALLEGIANCE: THE SPIRIT OF DANIEL

In every age, the true Christian will face a moment when the kingdoms of this world demand a loyalty that conflicts with the Kingdom of God. The test may come through legal mandate, social pressure, or cultural conformity.

In such moments, we must remember the spirit of Daniel, who would not bow. We must remember Peter and John, who would not be silent.

We must remember Jesus Himself, who stood silent before Pilate, knowing that His Kingdom was not of this world—but that it would one day overcome it.

"Of the increase of His government and of peace there will be no end..." (Isaiah 9:7)

A Final Word

To be Kingdom-minded is not to withdraw from the world, but to invade it with love, truth, and liberty. It is to resist the siren songs of authoritarianism on both the left and the right. It is to speak boldly, live purely, and refuse to compromise the values of heaven for the expediencies of earth.

So then: live in liberty. Defend the sovereignty of every soul. Trust God to do the transforming work. Be the leaven. Bring the Kingdom.

A CHRISTIAN MANIFESTO OF LIBERTY

Liberty is love. God is the author of both.

1. God Is the Author of Liberty

Liberty was God's design from the beginning. He placed the tree of the knowledge of good and evil in the garden, not to trap humanity, but to grant us the dignity of real choice.

2. Love Requires Liberty

True love cannot exist without the freedom to choose. Coerced love is no love at all. God invites, He does not force. The same must be true of His people.

3. Liberty Is the Soil Where Faith Grows

Faith that is not freely chosen is meaningless. God honors personal sovereignty—even when misused—because only free will can receive Him in spirit and truth.

4. God Delegates Authority, but He Is Not an Authoritarian

All legitimate authority flows from God and must operate with restraint, humility, and a servant's heart. Authoritarianism—power used to dominate or coerce—is a distortion of God's character.

5. Consent Is Sacred

God never overrides consent. He does not violate the will of those He created. Therefore, Christians must never use force—political, social, or religious—to compel belief or behavior in others.

6. The Kingdom of God Advances by Invitation, Not Coercion

Jesus did not seize power or legislate holiness. He proclaimed the Kingdom, loved the outcast, and invited people to follow Him. The Church must do the same.

7. Civil Government Has Limits Under God

Human government exists to restrain evil, not to redefine good. When government punishes the innocent or controls the conscience, it exceeds its God-given authority.

8. Taxation Without True Consent Is Theft

When a majority compels a minority to fund what violates their conscience, the principle of consent is broken. Coerced generosity is not charity—it is confiscation.

9. Private Property and Personal Sovereignty Are God-Given

Our bodies, our labor, our earnings, and our property belong to us under God. No person or state has the right to override that stewardship apart from justice or defense.

10. Authoritarianism in the Church Is a Betrayal of the Gospel

Christians are called to serve, not to dominate. From the Inquisition to modern cults, every abuse of spiritual power contradicts the servant-leadership of Jesus.

11. Revival Awakens Liberty, It Does Not Enforce Morality

The fruit of revival is voluntary holiness and generosity—not legalism, prohibition, or theocratic rule. Laws cannot produce righteousness; only the Spirit can.

12. A Kingdom-Minded Christian Respects Boundaries and Refuses Coercion

We are called to live as salt and light, not as tyrants. We speak truth, model love, and defend the liberty of every soul to choose or reject God.

A CHRISTIAN MANIFESTO OF LIBERTY

ABOUT THE AUTHOR

Paul Garner is a writer, educator, and publisher. After retiring from a 40-year career in finance and technology, he founded Panthera Publishing. He has authored and produced dozens of books that encourage spiritual growth, historical inquiry, and civic understanding. His writing blends clarity, compassion, and scholarship to engage both believers seeking depth and skeptics searching for substance.

Paul brings a rare combination of teacher's heart and philosophical rigor to his work. He has taught students across a wide age range, from elementary school to adult learners, always emphasizing critical thinking, imagination, and a deep respect for truth. He is known for making complex ideas accessible without sacrificing their nuance, whether writing about the founding of the American republic, the early church, or the life of faith in the modern world.

Spirit of Liberty emerges from years of personal reflection and Biblical, theological, historical and philosophical study. It invites readers into a thoughtful dialogue between the human longing for spiritual understanding and the desire to live the promise of America's founding from a Kingdom of God point of view. Drawing on the Bible and history, Paul makes the case that liberty is God's plan for people but His people have not always lived this way.

He and his wife, Kitrina, share a deep love for God and His Kingdom

You can learn more about his work or connect through pantherapublishing.com.

OTHER BOOKS BY PAUL GARNER

YEARNING TO BREATHE FREE: SEEKING LIBERTY IN A WORLD OF AUTHORITARIANS

Liberty for the people is resisted by those in power throughout the world. Most often liberty must be fought for, sometimes with violence, other times with persuasion, but never does it come naturally. Authoritarians can be found in families, churches, schools, businesses, governments, and communities always seeking to have their own way over the choices of others. Some are sociopaths with no conscience. Some are self-righteous moralists. Others may be driven by their own fears and their fears become a tyranny over others.

This book is about that quest for liberty in this world of authoritarians. It is not intended to be a book of history, but it does contain a great deal of history describing the many crossroads where liberty had chances to prevail but rarely did.

A RATIONAL CASE FOR FAITH

What if faith and reason were not opposites—but allies in the search for truth?

In a world increasingly divided between skeptics and believers, *The Rational Case for Faith* offers a refreshing and deeply thoughtful invitation: to explore faith not as a leap into the dark, but as a courageous and reasoned step toward light.

From ancient philosophy to modern science, from the logic of Aristotle to the longings of the human heart, this book makes a compelling case that belief in God can be intellectually sound, emotionally satisfying, and spiritually vital. Whether you're wrestling with doubts, defending your beliefs, or simply seeking honest answers to life's biggest questions, you'll find clarity, challenge, and encouragement in these pages.

- Is it rational to believe in God in an age of science?

- Can faith withstand the scrutiny of logic and evidence?

- What do the greatest minds—past and present—say about belief and doubt?

- How do we live meaningfully when certainty is out of reach?

Faith without reason risks becoming superstition. Superstition is belief that is disconnected from rational foundation, relying on emotion, tradition, or fear rather than truth. True faith, however, is not irrational; it is deeply rooted in evidence, reason, and trust in revealed truth. When faith operates without reason, it can devolve into blind acceptance of ideas that lack biblical or logical grounding, leading to distortions of true Christianity.

AFTER ACTS

What happened after the book of Acts?

The pages of Scripture may close with the Apostle Paul in Rome, and John receiving Revelation on Patmos but the story of the Church was just beginning.

After Acts picks up where the New Testament leaves off, racing through twenty centuries of Christian history in a vivid, high-level survey designed for clarity, insight, and inspiration. From martyrdom and miracles to councils and crusades, from monastic chants to revival fire, this book traces the powerful, often perilous journey of believers who carried the message of Jesus to every corner of the earth.

Whether you're new to church history or seeking a fresh perspective, this "sprint" reveals how the same Spirit that filled the early Church continued to ignite hearts, shape cultures, and overcome persecution. Discover how faith endured empires, faced reform, and flourished across continents—and how that same faith now lives on in a global Church still writing its next chapter.

SCROLLS TO SCRIPTURE

The Bible is a book of faith not unlike a biology textbook. Readers of both were not present when the writers encountered phenomena. We trust that the words we read, written by others, are truthful to their experience. In the case of the words of the Bible, followers believe that the words were not just the experiences of the writers but also inspired by the Spirit of God, the Holy Spirit. In this book we follow the path of authorship and the transmission of the words of the authors and the Holy Spirit across time.

If someone believes in Jesus through the testimony of those who walked with Him, they must believe in the whole Bible. Reading the words of Jesus found in the gospels, we find that Jesus ratifies the narratives of Adam and Eve, Noah, Moses, Abraham, David, Jonah and more. In this book we will find that the passing down of these narratives took on many forms beginning with an oral tradition followed by frequent copying and translation of text. Anyone who believes in Jesus, must believe that not only were the original writings fully the Word of God, but also the passing on of the narrative by all means must be shepherded by the Spirit of God also.

BIBLE COMPREHENSION GUIDEBOOK A SPRINT THROUGH THE OLD TESTAMENT

What is the purpose of the Bible? What is it all about? The answer to that can be found in the scripture itself. The Bible is about God's plan to carve out of history "A People for Himself".

But you are A CHOSEN RACE, A royal PRIESTHOOD, A HOLY NATION, A PEOPLE FOR GOD's OWN POSSESSION, so that you may proclaim the excellencies of Him who has called you out of darkness into His marvelous light. 1 Peter 2:9; Deut 4:20

After these things I looked, and behold, a great multitude which no one could count, from every nation and all tribes and peoples and tongues, standing before the throne and before the Lamb, clothed in white robes, and palm branches were in their hands; and they cry out with a loud voice, saying, "Salvation to our God who sits on the throne, and to the Lamb." Revelation 7:9-10

Ths is a a high-level survey, a sprint, through the Old Testament of the Bible. There is a common misperception among modern Christians and others that the Old Testament is "old" as in replaced by a newer model. Some go so far as to believe that the God reflected in the Old Testament is mean and judgmental, not like the kinder, gentler Jesus of the New Testament. They may miss the heart of the Father reflected in many places in the scriptures preceding Jesus.

Consider, though, that Jesus taught about the Kingdom of God from these Old Testament scriptures. He talked about Adam and Eve, Abraham, Moses, David, Daniel, Isaiah, Jeremiah, and Jonah. He spoke of the scriptures being fulfilled in Him. These scriptures were all from the collection of books we call the Old Testament. After His resurrection, Jesus explained to His disciples all about Himself from the scriptures, from Moses through all the prophets.

BIBLE COMPREHENSION GUIDEBOOK A SPRINT THROUGH THE NEW TESTAMENT

What is the Bible about?

It is God's for all people to join Him for all eternity

But you are a chosen race, A royal priesthood, A holy nation, A people for God's own possession, so that you may proclaim the excellencies of Him who has called you out of darkness into His marvelous light; for you once were not a people, but now you are the people of God; you had not received mercy, but now you have received mercy. (1 Pet 2:9-10)

For you are a holy people to the LORD your God; the LORD your God has chosen you to be a people for His own possession out of all the peoples who are on the face of the earth. Deuteronomy 7:6

The New Testament is the revelation of how this becomes possible. It is the story of how God took the form of a man and revealed God to people, then gave His life to open the door to all who accept Him to receive eternal life.

With 27 different books, the New Testament is worth a deep dive to discover the messages that God has for us all. Even so that can take some time. Often we can spend so much time diving deep that we can miss the big picture. This book is a sprint, not a deep dive. In these pages, the reader will find the high-level view of the whole New Testament.

MATH COMPREHENSION: ESSENTIAL BASICS

Many students struggle with math. Most often it is because they did not strengthen themselves with the basic 4 operations of addition, subtraction, multiplication and division. All math depends on these four legs. Practice is the only way to ease the burden of new understandings. Each new math method requires one or more of these operations. If a student does not learn them as second nature they will always struggle, taking extra time and stress, and may conclude that they will never be good at math. As with all things in life we get better through practice.

Bill Gates is often perceived as an overnight success due to his immense accomplishments with Microsoft. Gates had access to a computer terminal at a young age and spent thousands of hours coding and experimenting. His practice equipped him to seize the moment when personal computers became a revolutionary industry.

Michael Jordan famously didn't make his high school varsity basketball team in his sophomore year, but he used the setback as motivation to practice intensively. Over years of focused practice, he became one of the greatest athletes in history. This shows that natural talent alone isn't enough—consistent, targeted effort is key.

Anyone can become a rock star at math with practice. This book is structured to help with learning the basics and practice. Practice will lead to familiarity and ease encounters with new methods and capabilities.

AMERICA COMPREHENSION FOR BUSY PATRIOTS: REVOLUTION

For the busy Patriot in middle school, this book combines reading comprehension with American history. Specifically, this book contains factual short stories of the revolutionary period in

America's history from the Boston Massacre through the surrender of the British. It includes the heroic efforts of the "Sons of Liberty" and the leadership of George Washington. It also includes the influence of John Locke's ideas on the writing of the Declaration of Independence. These are exciting stories that also strengthen reading and vocabulary skills.

AMERICA COMPREHENSION FOR BUSY PATRIOTS: CONSTITUTION

For the busy Patriot in middle school, this book combines reading comprehension with American history. Specifically, it contains factual short stories about the US Constitution from the Articles of Confederation through the Bill of Rights. It includes the philosophy about how a government of a free people should work, and the differences at the Constitutional Convention, the Federalist and Anti-Federalist papers, state ratification, as well as the first Constitutional crisis.

AMERICA COMPREHENSION FOR BUSY PATRIOTS: SUPREME COURT

The United States Supreme Court stands as one of the most powerful and influential institutions in the country. Established in 1789 by the Constitution, the Supreme Court has the final say on matters of federal law and constitutional interpretation. This unique role makes the Court a critical guardian of justice, equality, and the rule of law in America.

The Supreme Court's primary responsibility is to interpret the Constitution and ensure that laws and government actions comply with constitutional principles. This power, known as judicial review, was established by the landmark case Marbury v. Madison in 1803. Judicial review allows the Court to invalidate laws and executive actions that it finds unconstitutional, thus serving as a check on the powers of the legislative and executive branches

This workbook contains the details of 17 of the most important and impactful cases decided by the court over 221 years. Each case is followed by comprehension questions leading students to consider carefully the importance of the case. Finally, there is an Answer Key in the back of the workbook.

CLASSICAL COMPREHENSION FOR BUSY SCHOLARS: GREEK PHILOSOPHERS

The writings of classical philosophers significantly influenced the founders of America as they crafted the principles and structures of the new nation. Figures such as Thomas Jefferson, James Madison, and John Adams were deeply versed in classical philosophy and drew upon the ideas of thinkers like Plato and Aristotle when developing the foundational concepts of democracy, governance, and individual rights. Aristotle's reflections on the rule of law and the importance of a balanced government inspired the American emphasis on checks and balances within the Constitution. Likewise, Plato's vision of a just society and the philosopher-king concept underscored the importance of wise and virtuous leadership, which resonated with the founders' aspirations for their new government. The emphasis on civic virtue and the common good found in the works of these philosophers provided a moral framework that guided the founders in their pursuit of liberty, equality, and justice. This philosophical grounding helped shape the American ethos, embedding values that continue to underpin the nation's democratic ideals and institutions.

READING COMPREHENSION FOR BUSY SURFERS 9THGRADE

Stories and questions to help early teens learn to read for comprehension. Book contains short stories and longer stories followed by questions to help the teen learn to focus and question what they have read.

READING COMPREHENSION FOR BUSY DANCERS, 3RD AND 9TH GRADES

A collection of stories for busy middle school dancers designed to help the student practice comprehension. Each story, tailored to their interests and grade, is followed by questions about the content of the stories to lead the student to think and comprehend what they read.

READING COMPREHENSION FOR BUSY ATHLETES: 9TH GRADE

A collection of stories for middle school and 9th grade athletes designed to help the student practice comprehension. Each story is followed by questions about the content of the stories to lead the student to think and comprehend what they read.

www.ingramcontent.com/pod-product-compliance
Lightning Source LLC
Chambersburg PA
CBHW020411150626
46554CB00012B/600